WHAT I'VE LEARNED FROM ATTENDING OVER 40 INDY 500s

Lessons in Sales, Motivation, Leadership, Management, and Life in General

By Jeff Cowan

Edited by Marianne Tungate

Jeff Cowan's PRO TALK, Inc. Rancho Santa Margarita, CA
info@jcowansprotalk.com

Ordering Information: For details, contact the publisher at the address above.

Printed in the United States of America First Edition

UPDATE NOTICE:

This is an updated version of my best-selling book, "What I Learned from Attending Over 35 Indy 500s'…". I have updated it for two reasons: 1. Over five years have passed since I wrote that book and I have now seen over 40 Indy 500s'. 2. When my grandson was 9, he read the "35" book. After doing so, he asked why I had not written about some of the more recent races and drivers. He also wanted to know why I had not written about his favorite driver, Andre Rossi. With this updated addition, I have now done both.

In the end, I have added five more chapters to the original book. They are chapters 25 through 29. I hope that you enjoy these new chapters as much as I enjoyed writing them.

TABLE OF CONTENTS

This book is dedicated to my Mom and Dad for raising me in the shadows of the Indianapolis Motor Speedway and all of its wonderful rich traditions.

It is dedicated to my lovely wife, Candy, for putting up with all my crap for reasons I can't explain or understand.

It is dedicated to anyone and everyone that has made and continues to make the Indy 500 everything it is.

And finally, it is dedicated to the grandchild of mine that thrust their fist in the air from their IndyCar while crossing the finishing line on the 200th lap of a future Indy 500 and screaming; "I just won the Indy 500! Thank you, Pop, I love you! This one is for you!" Even if it never happens, this book is still dedicated to my grandkids for all the joy they bring me on a daily basis.

P.S. Thank you Shawna. We all know this book would have been impossible without all your help and the long hours you put into helping me get it out there.

INTRODUCTION

ONE OF THE EARLIEST MEMORIES I have of anything to do
with the Indy 500 was when my dad's cousin, Raymond Haas,
who was a cameraman for the local television station that filmed
the annual event, would come visit our tiny two room home in
Plainfield, Indiana. It was a very big deal. Raymond would bring a
big projector and a big screen, and he would play the race for us.
Back then, the race was never broadcast live or even rebroadcast
on television at a later date in Indianapolis or the surrounding
area. The only way you could see the race, if you lived in the area,
was to actually attend the race.

Being a lower income family, we never had the opportunity
to see the race live, so it was a huge treat when Raymond brought
the film over and played it for us. On our race day, mom would
make sure that my two brothers, sister, and myself had our baths
and were in our pajamas at least an hour before Raymond arrived.
Once he did and he got everything set up, it was race day (actually
night) at the Cowan household! We all sat there, eyes glued to
the screen, nearly breathless, as we watched the Indy 500 unfold

right in our own living room. It gave us something to brag about with our friends and neighbors, most of whom never got to go to the race live, either. From those earliest memories, the Indy 500 was much, much more than a race, it was an event. An event that would bring our family and friends together in ways nothing else ever did or does today.

During my childhood, as the month of May grew nearer, there was a sense of excitement and anticipation that something extraordinary was going to happen. That emotion is as strong for me today as it was back then. Race day draws family and friends together as everyone makes preparations. Lines are drawn based on your favorite teams and drivers. Annual debates are renewed. Bets are made. Parties are planned and the speeds and happenings at the track are watched and followed with laser focus. Many times, throughout the month of May, the local TV and radio stations break in on regular programming with the latest happenings at the track, as listeners wait anxiously for every bit of information they can get.

On race day, when I was growing up, starting at 6:00 am, every dad in the neighborhood would turn on every radio in the house full blast. The point was so that no matter where you were, you could hear the happenings live from the track. Each year, as the start of the race grew closer, people would emerge from their homes. Grills got fired-up, people would be outside washing their cars, playing baseball, volleyball, badminton, or just mingling from one neighbor's patio to the next. No matter where you walked, stood, sat, or played, the race could be heard loud and clear. Emotions ran high as drivers passed for position, spun out, went in and out of the pits, hit the wall, or had engine failures. People laughed, cried, yelled, cursed, argued, and cheered as the race unfolded over the typically blazing hot Indiana afternoon. I remember dad always taking any bet that allowed him to have money on A.J. Foyt. That was "his" driver. He would always bet me two dollars, my weekly allowance for cutting, trimming, raking, and bagging our one-acre yard. He got Foyt and I got the rest of the field. A fool's bet I always thought, but a bet that kept father and son tied together for an entire lifetime—pretty smart guy, my dad. We had lots of differences over the years, but race day always seems to make the differences fade away. As I think about it, some of the most serious and meaningful conversations I ever had with my dad seemed to happen during racing season. As a kid and still to this day, the most fun I have every year is certainly during the month of May. Back then, I would skip school with friends to go to a weekday practice. Today, I still enjoy drawing drivers from a race pool bet and getting to see a driver up-close. One of the best parts about Indy is renewing annual friendships. Indy is and continues to be far more than just a race to me and mine.

I sometimes think of the few who never made the connection with the race and the month of May. I feel sorry for them. I have forged hundreds of friendships that I annually renew at every race. The pure excitement of being part of, in some small way, the world's largest single-day sporting event and what is truly "The Greatest Spectacle in Racing" is exhilarating for me. The Indy 500 has made my family closer. It has made me happy and made me sad, sometimes both at the same time. It has made me cry, laugh, and shake my fists in anger. It has helped me to gain perspective and to better understand people.

Not just the people of our great nation, but people from around the world. Indy brings us all together to share in a common experience. In many ways the Indy 500 has helped to make me who and what I am today. For those who don't know or haven't experienced the Indy 500, this may all sound a bit weird, but for the many millions who grew up with stories and memories as I describe here, they know what I am talking about. My family and I are not alone, we are part of a very large family. Indy fans are just that. One big happy family. The sentiments and memories people have surrounding Indy are like no other that I have seen. No other sporting or entertainment event seems to have the effect that Indy does on so many. The fact is, the only bad thing about Indy is that it only happens once a year. When it's over, you are faced with having to wait 365 days until you can experience it and all that it brings once again.

Even though the Indy 500 is the world's biggest single-day sporting event and has consistently delivered entertainment to millions around the globe, the Indy track was originally built for business purposes. In the very early days of automobile manufacturing, the original investors, Carl Fisher, James Allison, Frank Wheeler, and Arthur Newby, built the track with the intention of it being a testing ground for a wide variety of new cars and technologies. The first Indy race was billed as a day of death defying entertainment, but was equally billed as a day for businesses to sell cars. "Win a race with your car on Sunday, sell your cars on Monday" was the mindset that proved to be true.

Prior to the building of the Indy track, the way in which most manufacturers tested their cars was to bring them to road rallies and races on public streets. It was costly, dangerous for both drivers and spectators, and highly unpredictable. The building of a closed course circuit for the sole purpose of testing these new machines was welcomed by all.

Although the track was, and still is to this day, used for that purpose, it did not take long for the investors to see that real money could be made both on and off the track, if they staged races. They raced hot air balloons, air planes, and motorcycles. But it wasn't until they raced cars that they caught the world's attention. They not only caught it, but they have kept it for over 100 years by breaking speed records, introducing new technologies, producing high drama, exciting spectacles, and world class racing.

It started out as pure entertainment for me, too. From the first time I saw my first race, I was mesmerized, frightened, on the edge of my seat, with my heart pounding, hoping and praying, in near hysteria when things got too close.

In the grander picture, the race has become so much more than an incredible day. It has become a place where I've seen and experienced things that have shaped my character, my business practices, and life philosophies. As you read further, you will see that the events of the Indy 500 have had the single most significant influence on shaping the values and ideas that guide my business. The discipline and precision necessary for auto racing is directly applicable to sales and sales training. It not just about the race, it's about the people who attend, the experiences shared, and my ability to extract life lessons by paying close attention to all of it. As the Indy 500 excites me, I am equally excited about my craft and getting the messages of salesmanship, motivation, management and life in general to everyone who wants to know.

A WORD FROM JEFF ...

I AM A MOTIVATIONAL SPEAKER, sales trainer, and author. Overtime, I have found myself telling stories about my experiences at the Indy 500. I would tell a story about something that I witnessed or experienced, and then I would explain how a lesson of some sort or another was learned by that experience. It became apparent to me, very early-on, that when I told a story and presented the lesson learned, people in the audience would perk up and become more attentive. I was able to transfer my excitement about Indy and its applicability to life to the audience. They always loved it and they still do.

People approach me after a speaking event and mention how the stories are the best part of the event. It makes sense. We are all trying to identify something "out-there" with something "inside" ourselves. It is no secret that experience is the best teacher. Even bad experiences can teach us invaluable lessons. The fact that my stories resonate with others makes sense to me. When I tell you something that happened to me, you will see that I am very much like you and that if my methods are based on true life experiences, they can and will work for you.

For years people have encouraged me to share these stories and their many lessons in a book. So, after attending over 40 Indy 500s and well over 200 Indy car races, I am ready to share these stories.

As I do, I hope you enjoy the stories, but more importantly, I hope you can learn from them, as I have. My experiences have taught me about sales, motivation, leadership, management, and life in general. These great races, the drivers, the team owners, the track itself, and the many support players have helped me shape the successful personal and business life that I so enjoy today.

It should be noted that the stories I share are as I remember them. I have done my research and I believe that the stories are 99.9% accurate. Here is why I don't say 100%. As with all events in life, if 10 people witness the exact same thing at the exact same time in the exact same place, there will be numerous versions as to what actually happened. It's the human element of perception. Here's an example. Five friends and myself were discussing the 1992 Indy 500 where Al Unser Jr. won by the closest margin ever. The fact that Al Unser Jr. won is never in question. But HOW he won it, can be and is debated based on what you thought you saw, where you were actually sitting at the track, and what you were looking at when it happened. In that recent debate, we even pulled up several YOUTUBE videos so that we could, once and for all, settle the score. After doing so, no one was convinced that what they believed was incorrect. So, keep that in mind, if you are big fan of the race and I describe a story and you think it's slightly different from what you remember. Chances are, we're both right.

One thing that cannot be debated is that I have learned an

incredible amount of life lessons from watching and attending the Indy 500. It didn't take me long to understand that I was watching world-class titans of business duke it out with their cars and drivers at speeds that stun. I realized that if I paid close attention, I could learn a ton, and I did. I also realized that I was watching the world's best drivers and athletes making what always seems like split-second, life-changing decisions that impacted themselves and all who supported them.

I learned that money can buy you the edge, but it's by no means a guarantee of victory. I have seen many cunning underdogs rule the day. I have also learned that only fools would depend solely on technology or a human being to stay out front and win. I have seen many fast race cars end up in the wall because of human error, but I have also seen many lesser cars carried by human gumption and will, by a driver who knew what to do with what they had.

I have experienced every possible human emotion one can at every one of the Indy 500 races I have witnessed. Indy brings that out of you. I have seen it bring my family and I closer together. I have met and continue to meet, new people and establish friend-ships that I otherwise would never have the opportunity to do.

New Hampshire, Dover, Phoenix, Homestead, Pikes Peak, Charlotte, Fort Worth, Fontana, Kentucky, Tennessee, St. Louis, Michigan, Nazareth, Atlanta, Iowa, Disney World, the Poconos, and a few locations that I am sure have slipped my mind, are some of the places I have visited because of my love of following the drivers on the world's best ovals. Through that travel, I have been able to take my family and friends to most of those venues and they in turn got to visit places they had only read about.

To this day, the Indy 500 helps me to get out of bed in the morning and face the music. From the early days of my career when I did not have two cents to rub together, I was motivated to make one more phone call, send out one more thank you note, and make one more sale, so I would have enough saved-up to go to Indy. When things are tough and I wonder why I am putting myself through the grind that I sometimes do, all I need to do is look up at one of the many Indy 500 pictures I surround myself with to remind myself about the payoff. Getting to go to the Indy 500, sitting in the best seats in the house, staying at the Conrad, drinking great wine, renewing old friendships, and sharing it all with my beautiful wife, is my reward.

I think if Carl Fisher and the original founders were alive today, they would be proud to see how so many millions are entertained by this great event. I also like to think that they may be more than a little amused to discover that a goofball like me has not only been entertained, but has been taught life and business lessons that have, in great ways, shaped who I am.

Whether you are a big fan, small fan, or not a fan at all of the Indianapolis 500, it makes little difference. This book will be of value to you. The lessons shared and taught here are lessons that are timeless and highly valuable for anyone at any age. I love talking about this event to anyone who will listen. I love sharing stories. As a matter of fact, you can rest assured, that should we ever meet, I will be more than willing to hear anything you have to say about Indy. Just don't do it on race day. Don't try to talk to me from two hours prior to the start of the race until two hours after it is run. It's my day. As a matter of fact, I had only one condition when I got married—don't die, have a baby, graduate, plan a wedding, or do anything else on race day if you want me to attend, because I am going to be at the Indy 500. I am selfish only on that one day, each year. I work hard and I am a giving person. But on race day, it's family time. It's friend time. It's party time. It's time to be entertained. It's time to watch the world's best defy death and it's time for me to learn something about life, business and ultimately, myself.

Ladies and Gentlemen! Start your engines! Start living life and let's start learning!

CHAPTER 1
HISTORY IN THE MAKING

IN 2012, THE LAST LAP of the Indy 500 heading toward turn one found two-time winner Dario Franchitti on the *outside* with ex-Formula One, Japanese driver, Takuma Sato, on the *inside*. Side-by-side they raced, as they entered turn one, a highly risky move that usually results with one or both cars smacking the wall. Only in a handful of times have the best of the best been able to pull-off this move while on the *outside*, as that is usually the car that does not make it. In the stands, hundreds of thousands of screaming fans were on their feet, leaning away from the track, as if by leaning back it was going to prevent the inevitable crash that everyone was bracing for.

Every race fan at the track that day knew, just seconds before, as the cars came off turn four heading down the main straightaway toward what would be the last lap, that it was going to be one to remember. We all knew that if Sato got around Franchitti, he would win. But we also knew that Franchitti was not about to make it easy. He wanted that third Indy 500 win so badly, he could taste it and he had a reputation of doing whatever it took to win.

Sato also had a reputation of his own for "leaving it all on the track" as they say. "Pass or crash" is how most fans described him because he had a history of destroying more than a few cars in the years leading up to this moment.

We held our breath in unison, as we all hoped both cars survived turn one and delivered what was sure to be a legendary final lap of side-by-side racing to the finish. It was not to be. In an instant, the two cars, travelling the length of a football field every 7/10ths of a second, touched. Sato spun to a greeting from the wall that resulted in an ear-splitting THUD. Franchitti miraculously maintained control and cruised to his third and final Indy 500 victory!

Fast forward to 2017, with only two laps to go, and it was deja vu. This time Sato had a razor-thin lead coming down the main straightaway on the *inside* line. Suddenly, as he looked to his right, he found the legendary, three-time Indy 500 winner, Helio Castroneves, side-by-side with him. They were literally less than an inch apart, as their rocket-like cars hurled them toward turn one at speeds approaching 232 mph. Both drivers were crowd favorites. The fans knew exactly what Sato was capable of, "pass or crash". There was no way he was going to back-off. The fans also knew what Castroneves was capable of. He was going to do what he was so famous for: bob, weave, intimidate, and hit it flat-out. Castroneves never backed down from a challenge. He was fearless. It was the Indy 500. It was his shot at making history. Would his name be added to the list of the most prestigious group of drivers to ever win at Indy? A list that included such legends as A.J. Foyt, Al Unser Sr., and Rick Mears? These were the men whose claim to fame was that they were the only four-time winners at Indy. Would Castroneves's name be added among them? It was his best opportunity to date to make that happen. He knew it, and so did every race fan in the stands that day.

To say the tension was high would be a massive understatement. We were either going to see Catroneves do what he had done three times prior and win for an historic fourth time or, we were going to witness the crowning of the first Asian-born driver as victor at the Indy 500. As the cars reached turn one, still side-by-side, the crowd once again, took a collective deep breath, leaned back, winced, hoped, prayed, yelled, gnashed their teeth, and cheered to the top of their lungs, knowing they were witnessing history in the making. Indy fans love being a part of history and they absolutely loved what they were seeing at this momentous occasion in racing. All were nearly in hysterics as the drama heightened, waiting with baited breath as the final moments of the race unfolded in what seemed like slow motion right before our very eyes!

BUT WAIT . . . before I can finish this or any of the stories and lessons that will follow, you must understand that that none of this world-class racing spectacle would have been possible, if not for another brave soul, a businessman with the courage to dream big and the determination to make those big dreams a reality.

CHAPTER 2
TONY HULMAN

I CAN ONLY IMAGINE WHAT Tony Hulman thought as he walked onto the hallowed grounds of the dilapidated, run-down Indianapolis Motor Speedway in 1945. Grandstands collapsing, weeds growing two-feet-high through the once pristinely paved racing surface, and faded, chipping paint on what were once meticulously kept buildings was surely the sight that greeted him. During World War II, due to rubber and gasoline rationing, the track sat idle from 1942 to 1945.

Many others walked those same grounds at that time and pondered the future of the neglected stadium and race track. It had once been the international beacon of all that was automotive invention, but it appeared as though it's time had passed. Would it be best to turn it back to the lush farmland it was before the track was built? Should it be sub-divided for new developments and neighborhoods? Perhaps it should be the site of a new strip mall or industrial park. Its fate was unknown. Well, almost.

No, when Tony Hulman walked those grounds, he saw only one thing—opportunity. I like to think that what he envisioned and heard that day were thousands of screaming fans in *new* grandstands, *bigger* and *better* than any other sporting venue on the planet. He surely heard the mighty roar of the 33 high-speed chariots as they screamed into turn one on the opening lap of what he always viewed as the "Greatest Spectacle in Racing". He must have seen the thousands of spectators standing in approval and amazement as the drivers wrestled their machines with brute strength, wheel to wheel into the short chute, leaving all who were witnessing it breathless. He must have imagined the deafening sounds and the burning of nostrils that the opening laps always produce as fuel and oil take over the air. Of course, this is my idea of what he was thinking, but I know I can't be too far off the mark because Mr. Hulman seized the opportunity, an opportunity to not only rekindle a national institution, but to create a legacy, and bring excitement to millions.

I can only guess about how the players were feeling when, several days later, Hulman met with the then current owner, World War I flying-ace, Eddie Rickenbacker, at the prestigious Indianapolis Athletic Club in downtown Indianapolis (on Vermont and Meridian street for those of you who need this kind of detail) to sign the deal to take ownership of the track. The emotional conflict must have been incredible.

On one side of the table you had Mr. Rickenbacker. He was probably feeling somewhat relieved knowing that a huge burden was being lifted from his shoulders. There must have been tremendous excitement, too, at the prospect of the once great track being reborn along with his legacy. He must have felt, on some level, that he was getting the better end of the deal and that bringing back the race in all its glory was a real longshot. He may even have felt that Mr. Hulman was being a bit foolish. Perhaps he thought Hulman was making the decision to purchase the run-down race track more with his heart and less with his head.

On the other side of the table was Mr. Hulman. I'll bet he could not believe his luck in only paying $750,000 for such a hidden gem. This was the same exact amount that Mr. Rickenbacker had paid for the speedway back in 1927, when he purchased it from the original owners headed by Carl Fisher. This was when cars were racing at about 114 mph. Hulman certainly thought Rickenbacker was getting the short end of the stick. After all, who would want to part with something so grand and something that meant so much to so many? He was purchasing a piece of Americana, a piece of history.

I have often wondered, if on that day, did Mr. Hulman imagine the future? Did he, in his wildest dreams, believe that he would be contributing to an American institution that would last over 100 years, producing high drama, innovation, entertainment, speed, technology, and all the other benefits that the Indy 500 brings to thousands each year? I usually only wonder for a few seconds because I just know he did. He was a man of great vision and fortitude. I think he knew very well on that fateful day exactly what he was doing and exactly what was going to happen. Now, I do not know this to be fact, but I do so enjoy believing that his vision from the very start was to create greatness. I don't think he would be surprised at all by the success of the Indy 500 or the important role it plays in so many people's lives. He was used to winning. He was a man of vision. A man of vision who was accustomed to making the pictures in his mind become a reality.

LESSON LEARNED

In life, you must have vision. You must be willing to look at every possibility, new or old, and not step over those possibilities because hidden gems are everywhere. Even if you are successful at what you do, you can never really know what may be waiting for you around the next turn. You must keep an eye out for the next great thing in your life. It could be right in front of you. With vision, if you are currently struggling, you will have the ability to look beyond the stumbling blocks and truly see the bigger picture. Hopefully, a picture that allows you to change direction and find your success. If you are currently successful, then having vision can guide you to even greater heights. It's no secret. Everyone has greatness in them. Your vision has to include you being great at something. If you can't envision it, how will you ever be able to get others to see it?

PERSONAL STORY

A few years back everyone in the sales training business started converting their training from DVD's to online. Online was clearly the future and where the real forward-thinkers were heading. I quickly moved to the online format. I was actually the first to go in that direction in my line of training. It was a smart move. I doubled my recorded training sales within one year. No more

DVD's. Online only. It's what everyone did. After nearly ten years of not offering my training on DVD's, I discovered something interesting. As I traveled around to present workshops and keynote addresses, I noticed that nearly every training room I walked into had DVD players. Sitting beside those DVD players were libraries of training DVD's. You see, unlike DVD's of your favorite Hollywood movies, training DVD's are produced in a finite number. When they are gone, they are gone. It became apparent to me that people were years away from completely discarding their DVD's and their DVD players. The many sets of DVDs' that they owned were never going to be transferred to the online format. When I had this revelation, I shared it with my trainer peers. They all thought I was wrong and that producing DVD's would be like moving backward in time. I disagreed. I produced a small quantity of DVD sets, advertised them and sold out almost immediately. It's been five years now and I still offer my training on DVD and it accounts for about 5% of my sales each year.

Points to Ponder

You need to constantly be creating and editing your vision. Don't be afraid to look back at things. Don't have tunnel vision. Look everywhere for inspiration. History is a great teacher and from the past, we can absolutely pull information to guide us to the future. Create a vision, yes, but don't cast it in stone. A little tweak here and there and who knows? Have the fortitude to act and charge ahead. The sky's the limit!

CHAPTER 3
I'M GOING TO THE INDY 500!

"I AM GOING TO THE INDY 500!!!" I shouted it from the roof-tops. I yelled it and screamed it to anyone who would listen. I, Jeff Cowan, was going to the INDY 500! I was beyond shocked when my new boss of only 18 months called me on the telephone and personally invited me to go with her, her husband, children, and several of her friends to the INDY 500! This was as big a deal as had ever happened to a then, scrawny twenty-something, recently-divorced, had-just-lost-everything, not-sure-where-I-was-heading-in-life, guy from Indiana.

When the big day arrived and we were approaching the cathedral known as the Indianapolis Motor Speedway, I was not prepared for what was about to happen. I knew this event was going to be huge, but I truly had no idea. I had been to the track plenty of times to see the cars practice. I had even been there for qualification day a few times. Those are days when you may have five to ten cars on the track at one time, but they are spread out and not always at speed. Impressive, but nothing like race day.

The pageantry before the race which takes two hours to

complete and leads up to the actual start of the race was nothing short of mesmerizing. With each step, the excitement grew and the tension increased. From the second we took our seats, I knew this was not going to be just another day at the track. I knew I was about to be introduced to something that was going to change my life forever.

When the time came and the command was given to start the engines and I heard the mighty roar of all 33 cars firing up their engines, I was unsure if I was going to be able to contain myself. I was not alone. The 300,000 people around me were experiencing the exact same rush. When the cars started to roll and the parade and pace laps happened, seeing those 33 cars lined-up in eleven perfect rows of three, making their way around the track was nothing short of a spectacle. But how was I to know that this spectacle was just a teaser compared to the much bigger spectacle I was about to witness over the next three hours.

When the cars came off the fourth turn in perfect form in their eleven rows of three, already racing to the green flag for the start of the race, I knew right then and there that I was hooked—body and soul! I was all in! This was the missing piece. This is what I had been looking for. This was my reason, my purpose, and my passion. I knew right then and there that I would be coming back every year for the rest of my life, if God saw fit.

Several laps into the race, I looked over at my boss, the kind owner of the furniture store who was good enough to invite me to be her guest. She had a gigantic smile on her face as she thrust her fists in the air. Victory! She had accomplished her goal, and her goal was not simply to bring me to the race for a day of fun.

She was and had been looking for a way to motivate me, get me focused, and get me excited about something—anything in life. She was looking for something to fuel me to new heights. She believed that I had greatness in me, she just had to figure out what button to push. She realized on that day, and so did I, that Indy was it.

LESSON LEARNED

As a leader, you must motivate. Sometimes that means discovering and uncovering what it is your team really wants. What matters to them? What is important to them? Once you figure it out, it is your job to put them in a position to accomplish their financial goals so that they can acquire that which matters most to them.

PERSONAL STORY

Eighteen months before the day I saw my first Indy 500 race, Bev, the wonderful boss who treated me to the experience, had hired me. It was shortly after I had been fired from a shoe store where I was a manager. I got fired because I had a bad habit of opening the store late. The last year I worked at the shoe store also saw me get divorced from my high school sweetheart, whom I adored. The problem there was that I didn't adore her boyfriends and they didn't adore me. I discovered alcohol, drank myself to sleep most nights, and irresponsibly showed up late to the shoe store most mornings.

Shortly after being hired, Bev and the other managers quickly recognized that I could sell. I was capable of selling a lot of furniture, while holding on to a lot of gross profit. I think they thought I was some kind of prodigy or something. Truth is, upon being hired, I simply took their internal, highly professional sales class. I listened to what they told me would work and I did it. I felt like it was more them than me, but why tell them that?

The problem with my new-found success was that I was now able to make 200% more income than I had at the shoe store. I would have a great month and then the next month would sell next to nothing. You see, I wouldn't work as hard because I didn't have a need for all that money.

Bev was no dummy and had seen this same thing happen many times before. Her solution: Help me to find something that I would want to spend my money on or need to spend my money on and then put me to work to make that money. She was brilliant. She had detected that I liked "big events", like concerts for example. Her strategy included taking me to the biggest single day sporting event in the world. It got me hooked and gave me a reason to make the type money I did in the months I worked at my peak. She then gave me the opportunity to make what I needed and then some. It is expensive to go to Indy and sit in the best seats. The Indy 500 help me launch, in myself, the grit, determination and purpose that had been missing from my young life. Now, finally, I had what I needed to race through life at speeds I never dreamed possible.

POINTS TO PONDER

In order for employees to reach their potential, there must be motivation. People will make enough money to pay for the things that they want or need. Only personal tragedy or the desire to acquire will spark people to make more. As a manager, you have to figure out what "sparks" your employee. Essentially, you are helping them to create a vision for themselves and their career. Great leaders do this very effectively. If you work at it, you can be great at it, too.

CHAPTER 4
A.J. FOYT

A. J. FOYT HAS BEEN voted many times over as the best-ever to drive a race car, and by the year 1977, most of all the things that would make the world say that about him had already happened. Th ose accomplishments included wins in three Indy 500s, the Daytona 500, the 24 Hours of Daytona, the Firecracker 400, and the 24 Hours of Le Mans. But in 1977, at the age of 42, he proved to the world he was far from fi nished. At an age when most walk away from the sport or are pushed-out, he did the unthinkable and accomplished a feat that would solidify him as undeniably, the *best-ever*. A. J. Foyt became the fi rst four-time winner of the Indy 500. Even more remarkable was that he did it in a car that he built himself, something big-time drivers just don't do. Foyt went on to drive a total of 40 Indy 500s, retiring from driving in 1993 at the age of 58, breaking many more records along the way. As a matter fact, when A. J. walked away from racing, he held the USAC career wins record with 159 victories, he had won the International Race of Champions all-star racing series twice, accumulated a record setting 67 IndyCar wins, seven IndyCar championships, and was named driver of the 20th century. Although his family and friends encouraged him to retire up to 1977, Foyt did it his way. He drove until he no longer wanted to drive. In 1999 he was part of an Indy 500 win as a team owner. What's even more interesting is that not only did Foyt build the car that he won Indy with in 1977, but, from 1965 on, he also built nearly every race car that took him to victory. A. J. Foyt was in control of his destiny and always did it his way, under his terms. His stamp was on everything he did throughout his legendary career.

LESSON LEARNED

Take control of your career so that you may control the results. Don't be limited by the parameters established for you by someone else. Of course, we all need guidance, advice, and training, but what sets great people apart from average performers is that they take advice and make it their own. They figure out what works best in accomplishing the vision they have set for themselves. Personalize your business plan to meet your goals and aspirations and you will always remain in control of your business, but also of your career, your goals, and your future. There is nothing more freeing than truly being in charge of your own destiny. It's not easy to get there, but don't we all long to say, "I did it my way"?

PERSONAL STORY

Throughout my selling career, being number one was never my top priority. Although, with all due modesty, I was usually number one. For me, it was about the control and power I had over my career and my life by being a top producer. I noticed early on that extra time off, special assignments, leverage, and high income went to those who produced or sold the most. The more I sold, the more I got what I wanted, when I wanted it. I never abused this, but I did use it when I needed to. The simple fact in sales is that, the more you produce and sell, the greater control you will have over your career and your life. It was hard work, but the payoff was worth the extra effort. I became the master of my future and ultimately, I answered to myself. I was working to accomplish *my* goals, and that was, and still is, the greatest motivator in the world.

POINTS TO PONDER

One of the best things about being the number one salesperson is that people care when you get sick. What I mean by this is that it's important for people to miss you when you don't show up. A. J. Foyt was a leader in racing. When he was present, great things happened. Today, many still talk about how the racing world lost so much when A.J. retired. How terrible would it be to be in a job where nobody noticed when you stayed home? Top producers are valued and revered. Everybody looks to them for leadership, guidance, and ideas. When top producers show up, great things happen. Everybody wants to emulate winners. It's human nature, and we all have it in us to be winners. Take ownership of your future. Take that one extra step that others are unwilling to take.

CHAPTER 5

"I WOULD NOT RUN THE RACE IF I DID NOT FEEL I COULD WIN"

I REMEMBER THE 1992 INDY 500 like it was yesterday for three reasons. First, it was the coldest race day in the entire history of the race before or since. When I say cold, the concession stands at the track were selling coffee on a stick! Second, for some dumb reason, I invited my ex-wife from a decade earlier to be my date. The problem was, I still adored her after all that time, but she still had all those boyfriends that I didn't adore. (Note: I have not seen her since that day. Probably a good thing, since I assume my current wife and love of my life, who is 100 times the woman my first wife ever was, would not approve.) Third, because my favorite driver at that time, Al Unser Jr., won the race by the closest margin ever. He won it by just 0.043 seconds! But that's not what was, and still is, amazing about this particular Indy 500. It is the *way* that Unser Jr. won it.

It was Little Al's tenth attempt at trying to win the Indy 500. For years he had been the favorite driver of many race fans. What made this so memorable is that although most expected him to win the Indy 500 at *some point*, no one expected him to do it on *that day*. Everything was stacked against him: a record ten past Indy 500 champions in the field; weather so cold they almost postponed the start of the race; driving an untested car on the big oval at high speed for 500 miles. Most felt he and his team-mate Danny Sullivan would be lucky to make it to the halfway point. On the morning of the race, Al Junior was interviewed over the public-address system. When the reporter asked him what he thought his chances of finishing the race were, Al Jr. said without hesitation, "I feel my chances are excellent that I will not only finish, but win. I would not drive the race if I did not feel I could win. Indy is all about driving hard, giving it everything you got, and being a little lucky. I feel really good about my chances today."

Even after that statement, most still felt that Little Al had little chance to win. However, as the race began to unfold, it started to look like he really did have a shot at victory. As the race roared on we saw five former winners crash: Tom Sneva, Rick Mears, Emerson Fittipaldi, Mario Andretti, and Arie Luyendyk. Gordon Johncock blew his engine by lap 135. Of the four remaining champions that day, only one finished on the lead lap with him. It was his dad, Al Unser Sr. and he was ten-seconds back in third place. His teammate, the 1985 winner, Danny Sullivan finished fifth one lap down, as did the 1986 winner, Bobby Rahal. The great A. J. Foyt was the only other past champion still running at the end, five laps down in 9th place. If that was not impressive enough, the field day also had two future winners in it, Buddy Lazier and one-time Formula One driver, Eddie Cheever. Between all of those mentioned here racing against Little Al, by the end of their collective careers, these past and future champions amassed 24 Indy

500 wins, that's not including of course, his own two titles he won before retiring. What Al Unser Jr. did that day was no small feat. If, on that day, no one else believed he could win, what did it matter? He believed. He drove hard that day. He gave it everything he had and he got that little bit of luck he was looking for to win the closest Indy 500 ever. He won by a mere 0.043 seconds over second place finisher Scott Goodyear and ten former and two future Indy 500 winners. All this happened on a day that was as cold as hell, as I sat beside an ex who was just as cold.

LESSON LEARNED

Believe in yourself. Even when it seems no one else believes in or shares your vision, you have to own it. You must believe in your greatness, if you are going to achieve it. No champion has ever accomplished their goals by listening to naysayers. Champions and leaders have razor-sharp focus. I would have never achieved my goals if I listened to the negative people in my life and ignored my own vision. I had to keep my eye on the ball, with intensity and conviction.

PERSONAL STORY

Through Al Unser Jr's achievement and the achievements of others like him, I have learned to tune out the doubters. I have learned the importance of focus. I have had to shut out the world at times to get where I wanted to be.

Consider the following examples:

- "You should not sell furniture. It won't take you anywhere." was what everyone told me. Well, I became salesman of the year my first full year selling furniture. I moved into management and eventually became company trainer.

- "You will never get to sit in the penthouse suites in turn one at Indy." I did and have for over 30 years now.

- Everyone told me, "Candy Miller will never go out on a date with you." She did and I married her, and it was the best thing that ever happened to me.

- I can't tell you how many people told me that I was a fool to start my own business. I have been in business for myself for over 30 years now. My company, Pro Talk, is the #1 service department sales training company in North America.

- "You can't write and you certainly can't write a book." Well, I guess I showed them!

- "Supermodel Kathy Ireland will never go out with you." Okay, so they were right about that one. But, I did get to meet her once at a VIP event. I saw my chance and I took it. She politely, holding back a laugh, said no in front of a room of about 50 people. This was many years before I met my wife, Candy, by the way.

Points to Ponder

If you don't believe in yourself, others will rarely believe in you. You must be committed to your vision and your goals. Simply believing in yourself is not enough though, you must act. You have to develop a plan that includes the steps you need to take to make your dreams a reality and then you have to execute. The vision is part one. The hard work to make that vision come to life is what sets the winners apart from the losers. Be ready to dust yourself off and start all over again because as sure as I'm writing this, you will need to do that many times in your career. If you're the kind that gives up after the first sign of difficulty, you aren't likely going to make it to the winner's circle. Laser-sharp focus, impeccable work ethic, and an unwavering belief in yourself is what it's going to take to make it happen for you.

CHAPTER 6
AL SR. IS A BADASS

SPEAKING OF THE UNSERS, AL Unser Sr. and his record-tying fourth Indianapolis 500 win in 1987 was the Indy 500s biggest upset to date. Th e former three-time Indy 500 winner had been released prior to the start of the season from Penske Racing after having driven the four previous years with Penske. Roger Penske elected to run with drivers Rick Mears, Danny Sullivan, and Danny Ongais instead. Big Al decided he would go to Indy anyway and look for a ride to drive the world's most prestigious race. His plan was to fi nd a high-quality ride with a high-quality team within a week and if he didn't fi nd one, he would pack up and go home. Although he got several off ers to drive for some lesser teams, Al only wanted a car with what he thought was a winning team. No quality off ers were made.

Accepting his fate, Unser gave up looking for a ride, but he stayed at the track to help his son, Al Jr., get his Team Shierson Racer up to speed so that at least he could get into the fi eld.

At the same time, Mears, Sullivan, and Ongais were struggling with the brand-new PC-16 race cars that Roger Penske had brought to the race that year. They could not get the handling of the cars down or the needed speed and, during the struggle, Ongais actually stuffed his vehicle into the wall, injuring himself to the point of being unfit to drive. The PC-16 was so bad, Penske was forced to park all of the cars and put his remaining drivers into their year-old, back-up 1986 March/Cosworth machines. Now needing a third driver, Penske made a deal with Al Sr. He promised him a well-funded, year-old March with a brand-new Cosworth engine. Problem was, the car was being used as a show car and was parked in a Sheraton hotel lobby. Knowing that the show car was the same type of car that had won the past two Indy 500s, Unser took the deal. Missing the first weekend of qualifica-tions to get the show-car prepared, Unser got the car in the field on day three of qualifications and would begin the race from the 20th starting position.

From the start of the race, hardly anyone thought Unser had a chance. The field was filled with several past winners and Mario Andretti, the favorite that year, had a lightning fast car and led for a great deal of the race. But as the race progressed, everyone noticed Unser quietly making his way to the front. By lap 183, Unser had made it to the front of the field and the crowd of nearly 300,000 jumped to their feet screaming and cheering so loudly that Unser claimed he could hear them in the car. When he crossed the finish line that day, he became only the second driver, up to that point, to win The Greatest Spectacle in Racing four times.

What is even crazier about this and what most may not know is that this was not the first time he had won in this fashion. People forget that when he won his third Indy 500, he did it in a Chaparral/Lola. Although he started fifth that day, everybody thought his chances of winning were a long shot at best. His car was second tier quality to say the least. But by lap 75, he made his way to the front and dueled with driver Danny Ongais for many laps before Danny's engine failed. Once it did, Al cruised to his third title. He is the only driver in modern history to win the race twice in a car that was not of the current year.

Not done yet, he almost repeated these two earlier feats in the 1992 Indy 500 and in the process, almost became the only 5-time winner of the event. I have already described this race in a previous chapter—ten former and three future Indy 500 champions, coldest day, etc. None of that mattered to Big Al. Even though he began that race from the 23rd starting spot, even though he was driving for the underfunded Mernard Race team, and even though he was piloting a Lola/Buick on that day (the Buick engine being known for mostly blowing-up midway through every race), Big Al brought the car home to 3rd place only 9 seconds behind the winner that day, his son Al Jr. Many, including me, felt that if he'd had a better car that day, he would have in fact won for a fifth time. Al Sr. was always patient, understood the capabilities of the cars he had underneath him, and made the most of the hand he was dealt. He brought value, experience, and unwavering determination to every team he drove for and to every adoring fan that was lucky enough to get see him drive.

LESSON LEARNED

Al Sr., was a badass!! Just kidding. The real lesson here is that it's important to have the right tools to get the job done, but it is equally, if not more important, to have someone who knows what to do with the tools be in the driver's seat. Everyone involved in race car driving knows that having a spectacular car alone is not what wins races. It's what the driver and his team bring to the race that wins races. The car is just one piece of the puzzle. Experience, preparation, know-how, smart decision making, and focus are what lead champions to victory.

PERSONAL STORY

When I was just starting my sales training company, to say that I was broke was being kind. Knowing that the sales content I took to market would make or break me, I spent my first year putting 90% of my effort into creating it. In the process, I went through almost all the funding I had accumulated to start the business. It was supposed to have lasted two years. It barely got me through the first nine months. Inspired that year by what I had seen Big Al do, I practiced patience, I understood my situation, and I was confident with my ability. I knew I did not need to have the latest and greatest in office supplies to win. Instead of hiring a professional firm to create my materials for thousands of dollars, I hired students from local vocational schools who were studying such things and paid pennies on the dollar for their services. I went to the office where a girl friend worked and made copies when I needed them. I had my mom record the message on my telephone answering machine so that I sounded professional. I took an old briefcase and lined it with black crushed velvet in such a way so that when I displayed my wears, my manuals looked high-quality, modern, and expensive. The career I had chosen was loaded with large firms that had endless resources and cash. I went head-to-head with them many times on a three-day-old empty stomach. I did not win every time, but like Al Unser Sr., I won the big deals and the ones that most counted with the resources I had at the time. It created the foundation upon which my business still stands.

POINTS TO PONDER

To distinguish yourself as top salesperson, it's smart to create a brand that exemplifies quality, experience, and value. Keep this in mind from the very start of your sales career. Be creative, if finances are tight. Figure out ways to fake it till you make it. But, at the end of the day, your customers are buying you, and there's no faking that. On a related note, if you want to stand out with your *boss*, bring food into the office and lots of it, preferably the most fattening kind. You think I'm crazy? Try it and get back to me.

CHAPTER 7
NO RISK, NO REWARD

THE YEAR 1989 SAW ONE of the most exciting finishes ever in Indy racing. Two-time Formula One champion, Emerson Fittipaldi, had come to Indy a few years earlier to win the Greatest Spectacle in Racing. After several failed attempts, it looked like 1989 would finally be his year. Emerson's car was fast that day, as he held a lead for most of the race. However, with only seven laps to go, out of nowhere it seemed, Little Al Unser Jr. appeared in Emerson's rear-view mirrors. For two laps, Little Al harassed Emerson before finally taking the lead with five laps to go. For the next three laps, Little Al pulled away from Emerson with his only concern being fuel—would he have enough? Then suddenly, with two laps to go, while exiting turn two, both drivers found several lapped cars just in front of them. The crowd of thousands, already on their feet, knew that they were about to be treated to a thrilling finish.

The two jockeyed their machines down the long backstretch until they were wheel-to-wheel, side-by-side, heading into the treacherous turn three. With Little Al on the high side and

Emerson down low, Little Al pulled slightly ahead as they entered the turn. Both knew that this was a highly dangerous move. They both knew that if two cars went in side-by-side, it was likely that neither would make it through. But they also knew that there was a miniscule chance that one of them might make it and, being risk takers, neither one backed-down. In a millisecond, they both decided to not let up, and they each pushed harder. Carrying too much speed into the corner, the cars touched and Little Al spun into the wall, missing his chance at his first Indy 500 victory. With the race now under the yellow flag, Emerson cruised to his first Indy 500 win.

After the race, Little Al was interviewed and was asked what happened. Without an ounce of bitterness or regret, he simply said, "When you have two cars go into that corner, you know, at best, only one is coming out. With just two laps to go and an Indy 500 win on the line, you take that chance."

LESSON LEARNED

Nothing worth having comes without risk. You can't win or lose if you are not in the race. You must be willing to take a chance. Life is all about risk and taking chances. Two drivers took a chance that day. It worked out for one. It didn't for the other. But one thing is for certain, neither driver regretted putting themselves "out there" and taking the chance. If Emerson had not taken the risky move, it is likely he would not had been victorious that day. Furthermore, although Unser took the chance and lost, he learned a great deal. Three years later when Little Al got his first win at

Indy by the closest margin ever, a reporter asked him what was the one factor that most contributed to his win. Without hesitation, Little Al responded, "By losing the race three years ago, I learned what it took to win." So even though the chance he took in 1989 did not pay-off with a victory, it did provide invaluable lessons and experience which ultimately took him to two victories at Indy in the future.

PERSONAL STORY

I was raised in a family that largely did not take chances, especially in the area of career and finance. It was believed, nearly preached, that the path to a happy life was to find a good job, work hard, keep your mouth shut, take care of your family, and hope that things go well. I grew up in a neighborhood made-up of laborers, mostly, who all pretty much subscribed to the same mantra regarding life and career goals. But every once in a while, I noticed that people broke out. They moved up because they took a chance on something different. They broke the mold and reaped the rewards. I'm not saying that every person who tried a new direction was successful. Sometimes it worked out and sometimes it didn't. What made a lasting impression on me was that they somehow found the nerve to try. I always wondered where they got the strength to take those chances. Where did their confidence come from?

After I watched Little Al and Fittipaldi finish the race that day and listened to the interviews, it finally made sense to me why people who took chances were so willing to do so. It was because there really was nothing to lose. In Little Al's case, even though he took the chance and lost the race, he gained the confidence and experience that vaulted him to future victories. He had the peace of mind that comes with knowing that you gave something, everything you had. He "left it all on the track", as they say. After the race, win or lose, he was still going to be Little Al, the race car driver. A race car driver that had proven on other tracks that he could win and had proven that he was a formidable threat at Indy.

At a critical juncture in my career, thinking about that race helped me make the big decision to take a chance and start my own company. I could either be successful or fail. It was that simple. I got the nerve to try by realizing that, at the very worst, even if I failed, I was still Jeff Cowan the sales pro. I would still be a sales professional who could always make a living by moving a lot of product. Just like Al Unser Jr., I had nothing to lose and everything to gain. From that day forward, I put the pedal to the metal and drove everyday like it was the Indy 500 with just a few corners to go, allowing nothing to impede my drive toward my success.

POINTS TO PONDER

In my experience, there is actually very little risk in taking a chance. The greatest risk would be failure. At that point, you end up in your previous circumstances, maybe a little poorer, but definitely wiser. How bad can that really be? If you were surviving before you took the chance, chances are you will be able to survive afterward. I'm not suggesting that you take-off on some half-baked idea that you haven't worked at or investigated. Do your homework and prepare as much as possible. Work hard and know what you are getting yourself into. Do your due diligence. This won't eliminate every risk, but it will provide you with a sound foundation to take your chance and see where it leads you. There is no secret formula to eliminating risk entirely. If there was, I am sure someone would be selling it and making a fortune. But even bottling risk elixir would involve some level of risk, and somebody would have to take a chance on it.

CHAPTER 8
HUMILITY DELIVERS RICH BENEFITS

BEFORE WE STEP AWAY FROM the drama of the 1989 Indy 500 race, there is an important part of the story that I left out and it is definitely worth telling.

After Fittipaldi's and Unser's cars touched, it guaranteed "Emmo's" first Indy 500 victory. When Al Unser Jr.'s car cracked the wall, it came to a complete stop in the infield. Little Al then climbed from his car and hurried over to the edge of the track waiting for Emerson to cruise by on the final lap. The massive crowd was watching intently, wondering what Little Al was planning to do. The TV announcers were wondering, too. Was he going to throw his gloves at Emerson? His helmet? Something else? Was he going to shake his fist? Flip him off? As Emerson came by on the final lap with the race won, Little Al gave him the thumbs up, cheered him on, and clapped, as if to give him a standing ovation! By being so humble in loss, Al Unser Jr.'s popularity soared, and he became the driver everyone rooted for, for the rest of his career.

Likewise, that is why so many were always so supportive of the legendary A.J. Foyt. Although A.J. was known as a very tough guy who spoke his mind, caring little what others thought, he was always humble when it came to the fans, especially when it concerned the Indy 500. A.J. has said many times and continues to say to this day, "The Indy 500 made A.J. Foyt. A.J. Foyt did not make the Indy 500. If it were not for the Indy 500, even with all my other wins, no one would have known who A.J. Foyt was, nor would they have cared." Foyt's temper tantrums and antics were largely ignored by the fans because of his immense respect for them, the track, and most importantly, the Indianapolis 500. Simply, the way to win lifelong fans and unwavering support is to remain humble, no matter how successful you become, and always be respectful. It's the stuff your mom and dad taught you. It is tried and true.

On the other hand, one need look no further than Juan Pablo Montoya to see clearly how to lose fans and become a hated villain. Montoya came to Indy in the year 2000 and won. Although everyone knew they were going to get to watch one of the best drivers on the planet that day, by the time race day came around, most of the true Indy 500 fans despised him. We all knew he was an odds-on favorite to win. After all, he arrived at the race at a time when there were two factions of IndyCars: There were the better financed CART drivers who had not run in Indy in several years but had huge resources and teams, and there were the IRL drivers who were driving in the sanctioning body that included the Indy 500, but were driving with much smaller teams with substantially less money. All month long, Montoya was arrogant and cocky toward the IRL, their drivers, and the required IRL car he was "forced" to drive. As a matter of fact, on his first day at the track, he tactlessly put a John Deere tractor sticker on his car.

Although many big named drivers, including four-time winner Al Unser Sr., thought Montoya's cockiness would catch up with him during the race, Montoya put on a show that day, leading 167 laps and winning the race by a seven second margin over 1996 winner Buddy Lazier. He sealed his fate, though, as being one of the most disliked winners of all time in the winner's circle. After climbing out of his car, he was immediately asked what it was like to be the winner of the Indy 500. He smugly replied, "It's just another race." It seemed after that, the only fans he had around Indy were his team and a few CART fans. It was one of the few times I have seen a winner at Indy be booed.

When he returned to run the Indy 500 in 2014, he had added wins to his Indy title in Formula One and NASCAR. He was one of only three men to win in those three different disciplines. Mario Andretti and the late Dan Gurney were the other two. This time around he came in humble, having realized his past mistake and possessed an understanding of the true importance that Indy had played in his career. At this juncture, on a more level playing field, he was racing against many teams with similar budgets and resources. He finished 9th in the 2014 Indy 500. The next year he rebounded by winning a thrilling Indy 500. He was older and wiser and he described his win with words like "awesome" and "fun". His summed up the experience by saying, "I think what we saw here today is all the proof people should need, that IndyCar racing is the most exciting racing in the world. This is what racing and IndyCar is all about—awesome racing all the way down to the wire!" The fans went bananas and gave him their full support with loud cheers.

Lesson Learned

Being a champion is more than just getting your face on the trophy. It's being respectful of those around you and winning their respect through kindness and consideration for who *they* are. It is building enthusiasm in them and not robbing them of it. If those around you only become enthused when you fail, regardless of how much you win, you are not a true champion.

Personal Story

I hesitated as to whether I should include the Montoya story and lesson in this book. I decided to include it simply because Mr. Montoya and I have something in common; We are both recovering asses. Like Juan Pablo, in my early selling career, I was aloof, arrogant, and smug. I was good at what I did, and I knew it. When I was in the furniture industry and experiencing huge success, it was one of the best times of my career and one of the worst. I flaunted my success. I became the one everyone rooted *against*. The owners and management only put up with me and my attitude because I made them so much money. The "Salesman of the Year" award was handed out each year at a banquet. I can tell you with the utmost certainty that I was the only one who was excited about it. I can remember at one point, the Vice President in charge of sales asked me if I would stay in the banquet room long enough so that they could make the presentation. This was because I kept coming and going from the meeting throughout the night. I had made it appear as though I was just too important to sit there and wait.

On that particular evening, I realized by the way that people were reacting to me that I was a jerk. I was the butt of their jokes. I actually overheard someone say, "Don't be such a Jeff," my name replacing the word "ass" in their declaration. No one really wanted to talk to me. They only did so when they were forced to sit by me at dinner or stand next to me in line at the open bar. It was humiliating, and it changed me forever. As I was asked to come to the front of the room to accept my award, I had mixed emotions. I knew I had earned the award because I had worked hard and put in the hours, extra effort, and time developing my skill to achieve the distinction. But, it was empty. I had not stepped on anyone to get the award, but I had just not been humble on my journey. I decided, right then and there, that I was going to start *that night* to correct my ways. As I stepped up to accept my award, I did what I was instructed *not* to do and I gave a speech. The life went out of the room as people saw what they thought was going to be a gloating festival. Instead of doing that, I stunned them. For the first time since I began experiencing my success, I thanked them. I thanked the owners for the opportunity. I thanked my managers for their guidance. I thanked the deliverymen and warehouse personnel for all the hard work and effort that it took to deliver the furniture I sold. I thanked the office and finance departments for helping me with my paperwork. I thanked the buyer for having the eye to purchase the right furniture, and finally, I thanked the other sales people for putting up with my shit. I used that word exactly. I told them I had not realized their sacrifices until I looked at all of them and their spouses at that moment. I closed by promising to be a better person, a better teammate, a better employee, and ultimately someone they could count on. I told them I knew I had been a jerk and that although I was proud of the accomplishment, I was not proud of who I had become. When I finished, I got a standing ovation. It took the better part of the next year to rebuild my reputation, and it was during this time that I discovered that self-deprecating humor and stories were my new best friends, and they have been ever since.

Points to Ponder

Humility and its rich benefit to the quality of life is often overlooked today. It is always about being the best. Striving to reach your full potential and "getting yours". You see this especially in sales where the competition is fierce and the payoff for being the best is huge. The notion of being humble in sales in not an obvious one. As a matter of fact, a sales career requires high levels of self-confidence and aplomb. Humility and swagger don't initially appear to go together. But on closer inspection, it is clear that being self-confident and fearless is not necessarily accomplished without humility. As you progress in life and business you develop skills and understanding that allow you to properly engage in the right behavior at the right time. I have come to realize that for me, it is better to make myself the butt of a joke through self-deprecating humor and stories than it is to be the butt of everyone's joke because of my actions and attitude don't inspire respect. Winning is only fun if you can be a champion that people respect and admire. Winning and becoming a villain in the process will leave you feeling emptier than when your wife calls you by her newest boyfriends' name.

CHAPTER 9
IT'S NOT VICTORY UNTIL THE CHECKERED FLAG IS IN YOUR HAND

PANTHER RACING WAS BORN IN 1997 and had a long lineage of success in IndyCar. This was a team that took chances, hired aggressive drivers, and won a ton of races, including two IndyCar Championships by 2011. They were a smaller budget team. They knew how to get the most out of both their cars and their drivers. They knew what it took to make cars go fast. They had an eye for hiring some of the best drivers to ever drive an IndyCar. Panther Racing was a team that had a reputation for getting the job done with eyes wide open.

Having finished second in the Indy 500 in 2008, 2009, and 2010, to say that everyone was surprised when Panther hired rookie driver J.R. Hildebrand to drive their car for the 2011 season was an understatement. It was one of the most sought-after rides at the time and was usually offered to drivers who had already proven their mettle. Although J.R. had had an impressive racing career in lesser series up to that point, he was being handed a car that was fast and could win on any given day.

The four races leading up to the Indy 500 in 2011 showed

J.R. was steadily improving. He finished tenth in a race just prior to Indy, but many thought Indy would be a tough day for him. Throughout the month of May, J.R. listened to veteran drivers, took their advice, and stayed out of trouble. His speeds increased steadily throughout the month, and it looked like he would certainly be in contention for rookie of the year. When it came time to qualify, he delivered a speed fast enough to garner the 12th starting spot out of 33.

On race day, from the very start, J.R. quickly quieted his many doubters by staying on the lead lap and by briefly leading the race at the halfway point. He was proving that he not only knew how to drive the car, he also looked to be a master at conserving fuel, which allowed him to return to the lead of the race with just four laps to go. The crowd went wild as the crowd always does. Indy never disappoints and the fans knew, yet again, that they were seeing something very special. It would be the first time in many years that a *true* rookie would win the race. Everyone wanted Panther to finally succeed and win Indy. When J.R. came off of turn four and took the white flag signaling the final lap of the race, his team went nuts. Remember, Panther Racing had tried for years to win the race, having finished second the three previous years. Through their jubilation, they seemed to forget that their rookie driver was driving the last lap of the Indy 500. Instead of coaching him to the checkered flag, they started congratulating him and telling him to just bring it home. Through their excitement, they took their eyes off the ball and forgot to warn J.R. of a car slowing on the track in turn four. When J.R. came into turn four, the last corner of the race, he was surprised by the slower car just ahead.

This caused him to go high in the corner and hit the wall, ending his hopes for an Indy 500 victory. He had enough speed and momentum though to carry him across the finish line in second place, losing the race by about 100 yards. Many blamed the inexperience of the driver, many blamed the team for celebrating too early and being distracted. Some just chalked it up to how the track can giveth and just as easily taketh away. The crowd hung in stunned silence, but then . . . *To be continued in Chapter 10*

LESSON LEARNED

Do not assume victory until the job is complete and you have the checkered flag in hand. The last lap in any race is always the most important lap and many times the most challenging. All the laps leading up to the finish are important because they put you in position to win. However, it is the ability to successfully complete the final stretch that separates the winners from the losers. In sales, all the steps leading up to the "close" are important, but it is the final push that ultimately gets the buyer to agree and sign on the dotted line. The term "closer" refers to the person who can seal the deal, without loose ends or glitches. Closers don't take their eye off the ball for one second. They understand the importance of the final steps. Closers get paid.

PERSONAL STORY

Too many times throughout my career, I have seen business deals go south because someone took their eye off the ball at the most crucial point in the process—*the final steps*. I remember working on an agreement with one of my sales representatives that was coming together perfectly. It was not the biggest agreement I had ever put together, but it was significant. We wanted this deal to happen and worked very hard to get it. On the final telephone call, the client gave us the go-ahead. The sale was ours! We were to send the necessary paperwork and the client was going to sign and return it within 24 hours. Jubilation! My sales rep followed through and emailed the necessary paperwork. It felt good. Victory was ours! We were high-fiving each other while we prepared everything on our end so we that we could start shipping as soon as we received the signed documents.

But wait ... the next morning, there were no signed agreements in the inbox. Instead, I received an email from the client stating that they had not received the paperwork and that they were now reconsidering. Devastation!

As it happened, two critical mistakes were made. First, the sales rep did not contact the client after sending the email to confirm receipt. This is a safety net that I demand as I have discovered many times that just because you send an email, there is no guarantee that the email will be received. The second mistake was on me. My team was adhering to proper procedures. I did not reinforce my expectations. I relaxed too soon, and we almost lost the deal. On a business transaction of this size, I could not afford to make any excuses. Just like J.R. and Panther Racing, my salesperson "hit the wall" with just inches to go. Just like J.R.'s crew, I took my off the ball and did not coach when I should have been coaching. We had literally, almost celebrated our way out of a sale.

POINTS TO PONDER

A deal is not a *deal* and a sale is not a *sale* until the paperwork has been signed and the money has been collected. You can't build a resume or a sales career from the sales you *almost* closed. There is a point in a transaction where you will be very tempted to switch on the autopilot. I think this is a common pitfall for the experienced sales person. Just because it has happened for you many times before, doesn't automatically mean that your next deal is going to close. Treat each and every deal like it's the only one you've got. Follow through to the very last detail. If you are a team leader or manager, the buck stops with you. Save the celebrating for when the money is in hand. You cannot celebrate your victory until you cross the finish line.

CHAPTER 10
DETERMINED

So, TO CONTINUE WHERE WE left-off with our mini cliff-hanger in Chapter 9, now we will look at the racing savvy of Dan Wheldon on that fateful day in 2011. Determination is the only word that can explain how Dan Wheldon won his second Indy 500. When most drivers had contracts in hand to drive their cars months before the start of the racing season, Dan Wheldon found himself in a contract dispute with his then-current team. Just eight weeks before the start of the 2011 IndyCar season, the team Wheldon had finished second with at Indy in both 2009 and 2010 released him. With all the cars having drivers assigned to them at that point, Dan Wheldon found himself without a car to drive. But he was determined. When asked what he thought his chances were of driving that year, he replied, "Bleak!" But he was determined. He continued, "I am determined to have a car for Indy that can help to put me in the winner's circle, again." He and ex-teammate, former driver Bryan Herta, teamed up when Herta started a new team and hired Dan as the driver. New one-car teams rarely do well at Indy. But Dan was determined. He was determined to qualify for the race, and he produced a strong time, starting him sixth out of 33 cars. Wheldon was determined to be a contender throughout the entire race, and he was. Although he never led, he stayed in the top ten most of the day and was always right behind the leaders. He was unshakable. As Dan entered the final lap of the race, he was in third place and quickly made a pass for second place. He was determined. With the leader now in his sights off of turn three, just four hundred yards ahead, Wheldon was determined. Then, as the race leader and rookie driver, J.R. Hilderbrand, hit the fourth turn wall after trying to pass a severely slowing car, a determined Dan Wheldon passed him with just one hundred yards to go to the finish line and won his second Indy 500. In doing so, he became the only winner to win the race having only lead for one lap. He was determined.

Lesson Learned

Determination does not stop at the birth of an idea. For it to result in victory, determination is needed at conception, execution, and completion, for your goal to result in victory. Your determination must increase with each step you take toward your goal, if you wish for you goal to be realized.

Personal Story

Up until 2008, I was very fortunate in business. I worked hard, developed great products, created effective marketing tools, and sold a ton. I was doing exceptionally well, until September of that year. When the housing market crashed, people stopped buying cars. With over 80% of my products tied to automotive retail sales, everything stopped. Overnight, I lost the ability to generate new business, which had amounted to over half of my monthly income. To make matters more intense, eighteen months prior to this, I married Candy, purchased a large home in southern California, bought all new furnishings, purchased new landscaping, and was parking three brand new vehicles in the driveway of my new home. It was the most financially challenging situation of my life. Thanks to several long-term agreements that I had with a couple of manufacturers and to some very solid clients, I was able to pull through and survive until 2011. In 2011, as those agreements were coming to fruition, it was decision time for me. Did I double down and carry on, or did I accept one of the many offers I had to close my business and work for someone else? As I sat in Penthouse B in turn one in 2011, and watched Dan do what he did, I was inspired. When Dan, a past Indy 500 winner and past driver for some of the biggest and most successful teams in the sport, was at his lowest point in IndyCar driving, he did not walk or let his ego get in the way. He instead made a calculated choice. Even though he was driving with a brand new team running their first IndyCar race, he knew the car, the power plant, the owner, the crew, and the track. I can only assume he knew all the pieces were in place for a win-win situation. If he did poorly, no one would blame him. From the outside, he would be seen as a former champion, helping a former teammate establish a new team, a selfless act of giving back to the sport. People admire those who help others achieve in a field where they have excelled. If Wheldon was successful, it would provide the added bonus of putting his IndyCar career back on track. He was determined to not let his driving days end. He took the chance. Refer to Chapter 7 for the merits of taking a chance. It is almost always worth the risk.

It mirrored my situation exactly. If I doubled down in 2011, opened a bigger office, and brought on new people, it would be bold, but the pay-off could be tremendous. If I failed, I would still be the same guy who had accomplished what I had in the past. I would not be seen as a failure, as the challenging economy would surely be viewed as the culprit. If I worked hard and got a little lucky, I might be able to regain and possibly exceed my prior success. Either way, I would come out the other end. Either way, I would still be Jeff Cowan, sale professional, who could always make a living selling product. Like Dan, I really had nothing to lose. It was Dan's show of determination on that day that inspired me to keep-on keepin'-on. So many times, people give-up, one step away from success. I almost did. I credit my courage to the Indy 500 for inspiring me to keep my drive alive!

POINTS TO PONDER

Necessity, as the great philosopher Plato said, is the mother of invention. But it is *determination* that gets the invention to market and ultimately decides success. President Calvin Coolidge may have said it best when he stated the following: "Nothing in this world can take the place of persistence. Talent will not: nothing is more common than unsuccessful men with talent. Genius will not: unrewarded genius is almost a proverb. Education will not:

the world is full of educated derelicts. Persistence and *determination* alone are omnipotent."

The only time determination has ever failed me is when I have been determined to prove my wife wrong in an argument. Then, determination is futile, and surrender is the best and most prudent option. I bet even Calvin Coolidge would agree with me on this one.

CHAPTER 11
YOU DEFINE WHO YOU ARE

MICHAEL ANDRETTI HAS BEEN EXHILARATING, fun, inspiring, and interesting to watch throughout his entire career. Since he and I are about the same age, I compare notes on our lives. For instance, in 1983 while he was trying to figure out how to make his IndyCar stick to the track at speeds well over 200 mph, I was trying to figure out how to earn enough cash to keep my 1979 *'vette* running. Okay, it was a four-door, four-cylinder, manual transmission *Chevette*. So maybe our lives weren't exactly parallel, but like everything Indy, I felt a connection. I was astounded by what he was doing and what he was accomplishing. I mean this guy was fast out of the box. Coming to Indy with several championships and many wins in the lower series leading up to it, everyone knew this was a driver to watch. On top of all that, he is the son of racing legend Mario Andretti.

Over his driving career in IndyCar, he amassed 42 wins, putting him third on the all-time winners list with only his father Mario ahead of him with 52 and A.J. Foyt with 67. He won an IndyCar series (CART) championship and finished in the top ten in the championship standings 17 times. He won a single season high of eight races. Al Unser Jr. was the only other driver to accomplish that in IndyCar history. In 16 attempts, he led the Indy 500 nine times. He finished second in 1991 to multi-winner Rick Mears after the two made high risk turn one passes on each other in the closing laps of the race, giving fans a show to remember and a race still talked about today. In his first Indy 500 he was named co-rookie of the year. He finished his Indy 500 career having led the race for 431 laps, the most ever led by a non-winner of the event.

As his driving career was winding down, there was no doubt that he would be remembered for his last accomplishment—the most laps led *without* a win at Indy. He was even voted the best driver to *never* win at Indy. It looked like this would be his legacy. He would be remembered for the one thing he *didn't* do—win the Greatest Spectacle in Racing, the Indy 500.

But Michael had other plans. Those plans were what impressed me the most. He was not about to let his legacy be limited to how others defined success. Ironically, it appears that Michael Andretti will be defined as much by what he has done out of the car as by what he has done inside of it. Since ending race car driving, Michael has shown he was only getting started:

1. He bought an IndyCar team that has never run fewer than three cars and has as many as six, depending on the event.

2. He has taught his son Marco how to be fast at Indy. Marco finished second in his first Indy 500, becoming "Rookie of the Year", in a race that will be remembered as the second closest finish in Indy history.

3. He supplied a car to Danica Patrick. While driving for him, she scored the first win for a female driver in a major racing series. She was also the first woman to lead competitive laps at the Indy 500 (ten). She finished third at Indy, the highest finish for a woman.

4. In 2004, his driver, Tony Kanaan, won the IndyCar championship by completing all 3,305 laps run that year in the series, the only driver to accomplish that feat in any major series globally.

5. His team has dominated the Indy 500 in recent years, winning the event five times, tying him for second as a team owner. Only Roger Penske's team has won more. His team's last three Indy 500 wins were done in such dramatic fashion that once run, they became instant classics.

Instead of being defined by what he *did not* do as a driver, which was win the Indy 500, he took charge of his own destiny and will go down in history as a guy who won the Indy 500 as a team owner at least five times and probably many more. It is strange to think that those who are new to the Indy scene may never understand or realize how fierce Michael Andretti was as a driver because of his achievements as a team owner. He refused to be defined by a single accomplishment. He didn't rest on his past performances. He kept moving forward, always looking for a new challenge.

LESSON LEARNED

Many things will happen throughout your life, both good and bad. How others regard you will either be decided *by* you or *for* you. For me, it is far more desirable to take control of the direction of my life. Even if there is risk of failure, I am comforted by the idea that it was my choice to be on the road that I am traveling. I have always had a hard time letting others decide things for me. That's probably why I gravitated toward a career in sales that led to me to own my own business. Witnessing the lives and the struggles of some of the finest Indy drivers has given me the gumption to take a shot for myself. I have learned more about life and how to navigate the twists and turns in the road through watching my favorite drivers during their careers than I ever would have in any classroom.

Personal Story

Drivers like Michael Andretti inspired me by demonstrating a character trait that all truly successful people possess. They do not allow one singular thing in their lives to define who they are or what they can achieve. No one event or accomplishment is the sole focus of a truly successful person. Truly great people are the culmination of a lifetime of experiences: the good, the bad, and the ugly. Every year, I watched young drivers come into IndyCar racing. A few would make it. Most did not. Many drivers would come in, have a bad qualifying attempt, not make the race, and disappear, never to be heard from again. Some are forever remembered for their poor performances. However, there were a precious few like Michael Andretti, Al Unser Jr., Jacques Villeneuve, Scott Goodyear, Takuma Sato, and Paul Tracey who would never allow a single event to define them. Sure they may have been disappointed when they did not race well or take home the trophy, but in post-race interviews you could always tell that when they said they would be back, they meant it. Maybe not as a driver. Maybe as something else, but you knew they had more to offer the racing world. Just imagine how much less Indy would have been if A.J. Foyt had been satisfied with one win and retired. What if Little Al had given up in 1989 after his near win and let that define his career? And looking beyond the race-world, what would society look like today if after being fired from Apple in 1985, Steve Jobs gave up and let that experience be his defining moment?

I am sure in every one of these instances, there were many who told these people that they had done enough. No need to do anymore. No need to continue to push. No need to risk tarnishing what was already accomplished. It seems that nearly every big step I have taken in my life has been accompanied by countless people who have tried their darndest to convince me to not pursue my direction. Their plan was better for me. My high school guidance counselor thought it would be best for me to find a safe and steady factory job. I was told I was fool each time I left a successful sales job to expand my horizons. I was told as a consultant to focus on local business and not bid on national accounts. I'm sure their intentions were good, but you know what they say about good intentions. I certainly could have heeded the free advice and maybe I would have been happy. I'll never know. The one thing that always kept me from taking the advice of others was that *their* vision for my future never matched *my own* vision. I simply refused to let others define who I was, what I would become, the level of success I was going to achieve, or the contributions I was going to make in life. Making the tough decision to move on after a great success or a great failure takes nerve. There are no guarantees. You will always be remembered for what you have done up to that point in your life. You must decide to go for more or walk away. Either way it's okay, as long as *you* are making the decision. There is nothing wrong with seeking out the opinions and advice of those you admire and trust, just be sure that the final decision is yours. Don't allow others to limit your options based on their expectations. Follow your gut.

Points to Ponder

The high school football star that wins or loses the championship for the team in the last second of the game chooses to let that define them for the rest of their life, or they can choose to make that moment a footnote in their life history by refusing to let it define who they are. The salesperson that wins or loses the salesperson of the year award by a single point can let that define who they are and forever be remembered for that one year, or they too can make it a small footnote in their lifelong career. I have always tried to define who I am on my own terms. When I got married the first time at the ripe old age of 19 and then divorced 18 months later, I would not let that define who I was. I refused to be remembered as the divorced guy. Instead, I took charge and forever became known as the guy who won and got revenge. How? I let her new boyfriend keep her. That's how I'm defined in that situation.

CHAPTER 12
BEING AGGRESSIVE WINS RACES

MARIO ANDRETTI IS SYNONYMOUS WITH the word "winner". I was lucky enough to get to see him race and win several races on various tracks. All the way to the end of his racing career, if Mario was on the track, he was a threat to win. Th e only driver to win the Indy 500, Daytona 500, A Formula One championship, countless other championships and 109 races on major tracks, Mario was an aggressive charger. His hard charging and aggressive driving also cost him many races. For instance, he drove in 29 Indy 500s, but he only drove the complete 500 miles 5 times. "Mario is slowing down on the backstretch" became synonymous with the running of the Indy 500 during his time at the track because of how intensely and aggressively he drove his machines. One day while I was at a practice day for the Indy 500, Mario was being interviewed over the public-address system. Th e interviewer asked Mario if he felt his hard charging and aggressiveness had cost him some victories. Paraphrasing Mario's reply, as I remember it, he said, "Probably. But I am not paid to just drive cars, I am paid to drive them fast and win races. Th at has always been my style. I believe more drivers lose races because they back off when they are in front and stop doing what got them to the front in the first place. When they try to save the car, they slow down, and the way the car handles and performs changes. The track and conditions change. The driver themselves change. I would rather say I lost a race because I pushed too hard then to lose a race because I did not drive hard enough." The 1987 Indy 500 validated what he said. After leading 170 of the first 177 laps and leading the race by over two laps, his team told Mario to slow down and conserve the car. Mario did, and by doing so, his reduced engine rpms created a harmonic imbalance in his turbocharged Ilmor/Chevrolet V8 that led to a broken valve spring with 20 laps to go. Mario had to settle for a ninth place finish that day. Mario's hard charging and aggressiveness may have cost him a lot of races, but it won him more than enough races for him to become known as one of the best drivers to ever get behind the wheel of a race car. 1969 Indy 500 winner Mario Andretti's accomplishments are likely to never be matched.

LESSON LEARNED

You have to be aggressive every second of every day to collect the most wins. Being aggressive may cost you here and there, but in the end, you will have more wins that count than not.

PERSONAL STORY

The problem most people have with being aggressive is that they misinterpret what it means to be aggressive, have had a bad experience with being aggressive, or had a bad experience with someone being aggressive with them. Here is what I mean. I remember as a five-year old being very aggressive in play like most kids. I remember playing baseball in our backyard one day. My sister, who is six years older than me, was up to bat. I did not want to wait my turn, so I aggressively stormed up to the plate to push her out of the way as she was in mid-swing. She smacked me across the face, cracking my eye socket. Message learned, don't be aggressive in play and wait your turn. Running late to school one day at the age of 16, I put the pedal to the metal and, at 100 mph, aggressively weaved in and out of traffic to make up time. I got a $500 ticket, a ton of points added to my license, and my car insurance, that I had to pay for, doubled overnight. Lesson learned, drive like a fool and pay a big price. I could go on and on here with similar stories—being aggressive at the wrong time or in the wrong place has its price. But watching Mario, I learned that being aggressive was good and could get you what you wanted IF used at the right time in the right way. Mario was very aggressive on the track but was and is mild mannered outside the car from what I can tell. As matter of fact, he always came across to me as just being flat out "cool" in the "cool dude" sense.

Points to Ponder:

I learned from Mario that when I was selling and doing business were the times to be aggressive. Being aggressive with family and friends or in other situations usually have a very negative affect. In sales and in business though, you have to be aggressive or you will not survive and you will not win. I am often asked how one learns if one is not being aggressive enough or if they are being overly aggressive. Easy, with your paycheck on the line, ask for the sale repeatedly. If the client says yes after, it was the correct amount of aggressiveness. If you ask repeatedly and the customer says no, ends up not buying, and they display even the slightest bit of frustration or anger, you were maybe too aggressive. It may seem like a crazy way to learn, but it is the only way I have ever seen work. It is just like driving a race car. If you are too aggressive, you may hit the wall or blow your engine. If you are not aggressive enough, you will lose the race. Passive salespeople do not earn commissions or win awards. Salespeople that are aggressive, persistent and focused do.

CHAPTER 13
PITFALLS OF A SELF-SERVING ATTITUDE

IN 1993, TWO-TIME FORMULA ONE driving champion, Cart champion, and 1989 Indy 500 winner Emerson Fittapaldi was one of the most respected and beloved drivers in the world. His fan base was huge. Emerson was fun to watch drive as he was prone to taking high risks and making every race he was in highly entertaining. He won a lot of races and was always a fan favorite—until he won his second Indy 500 in 1993. With just 15 laps to go in the race, Emerson took the lead from another formula one champion, Nigel Mansell. The crowd went wild. As Emerson pulled into the winner's circle and removed his helmet, he was met with a standing ovation. Then in one very selfish move, he refused to drink the traditional milk that many Indy winners began drinking in 1936 and all have drank since 1956. Instead, Emerson repeatedly pushed the traditional bottle of milk away and refused to drink it, drinking orange juice instead. The crowd instantly turned on Emerson and began heckling and booing him. He drank the orange juice because he owned orange groves and wanted to promote it. He never recovered. From then on, for the rest of his career, he was booed. Even when he returned in retirement to drive the pace car for the Indy 500 in 2008, 15 years after the fact, the crowd still booed and heckled him. It took Emerson about 20 years to become a crowd favorite and less than a minute to become the villain of racing for the rest of his life. What is really sad here is he could have easily accomplished both: please the crowd by following tradition and drinking the milk, and promoting his business by returning later with a staged shot of him drinking orange juice in the winner's circle when no one was around. A possibly even smarter thing to do, I think, would have been to drink the milk, and then run an ad with a picture of himself drinking a glass of cold orange juice at a breakfast table with a second picture of him in the winner's circle drinking the milk with a caption that read, "My day ended with a glass of milk, but it started with a glass of orange juice!"

Lesson Learned

When serving the public, you must always put the public and it's interest ahead of your own.

Personal Story

This is not so much a personal story as it is an opinion. What Emmo, as he was known to fans as, did was un-American. The essence of being an American is putting your personal interest second and the interests of others first. That is exactly why we are so endeared to the first U.S. president George Washington.

Look at the sacrifices he made without ever asking for anything in return. He could have president as long as he wanted and was actually offered a lifetime term, but he turned it down for he felt it was best for the nation. The "Greatest Generation," who fought WWII and won, is considered to be the greatest because they made the sacrifice asking nothing in return. Same can be said for selfless athletes who play with injury so that the team and the fans get the win. We love these stories and love those types of people. Those who win and then accept their winnings humbly, thank the fans, appreciate the supporters, and respect tradition are the ones who are the true champions in life. It was stunning to me that day when Emmo did what he did. Not so much for the disappointment I felt, but because I knew, in an instant, what he had thrown away. Today, with social media, we have been accustomed to people blowing everything they have worked for with a simple text, Facebook post, or tweet. We are nearly numb to it. Although we may forget in the short term when someone does it, we never forget in the long term. Once your actions and words are "out there," they are out there and out there forever. Just like we always remember the sacrifices, we never forget or forgive the selfish.

POINTS TO PONDER

Having a self-serving attitude and approach to life will certainly not kill you, but it will ultimately kill any enthusiasm those around you have for you regardless of how great you are at whatever it is you do. One of the basic premises of the selling profession is to always talk about and present what the other side will gain and how they will benefit. Possibly the only type of person that is worse than someone who is self-serving and always thinks of putting themselves first is an in-law.

CHAPTER 14
IT'S A BUSINESS DEAL

THE INDY 500 IS A business first and entertainment second. The fans many times forget that. We get angry when a team releases a favorite driver or when a sponsor stops sponsoring a team. Sometimes the drivers that are released are those who never got a fair break with the right car or team. Sometimes it is big time drivers that have storied pasts and multiple wins. I will never forget how sad it was when three-time Indy 500 winner Johnny Rutherford tried to get in Indy for the last time and could not get his car up to speed. None of the big teams would sign him and the small teams he was trying to drive for just did not have what it took to make him go fast. Johnny was crushed and choked back tears in the TV interviews that followed. He had given it his all. The team had given its all. The passion was obvious. Same can be said for countless others. For one reason or another, a team releases a driver, and you can feel the disappointment as decisions like these are never easy and certainly never fun. Not fun for the team owners, not fun for the drivers, and most of the time, never fun for the fans. It's business.

One of the toughest firings at the track I ever witnessed was when the great A.J. Foyt, as a team owner, fired himself. In 1993 after a week of practice, Foyt saw his young hired rookie driver, Robbie Gordon, hit the wall in practice. A.J. knew his time had passed and that it was time to step out of the car, be a team owner, and help his other drivers get their cars safely up to speed. The passion A.J. Foyt displayed as he tearfully retired from racing as a driver in front of the crowd of 100,000 that day said it all. It's a business deal, you have to do what is best for the team. A.J., like so many other owners, knew the time had come to replace a driver whose time had passed. This time it was him. He was the driver. His time had passed and although he still had the passion, still had the drive, he did what all smart business and team owners do and made the tough decision. Made the decision that was best for the team. If you ever wondered what it is like to see 100,000 adults cry at the same time in the same place, watch that video. I still cannot watch it today without tearing up.

Other times drivers get to drive cars, and it does not seem fair since they have a questionable driving record and others with far superior talent are left standing on the sidelines—but again, it's a business deal. In Rutherford's case, it was crushing for his many fans. It made it real. In one bold stroke, it hit me like a ton of bricks. Racing is a business deal from top to bottom. Nothing more, nothing less. Drivers and race teams are not family and they are not friends in the truest sense. They are a business and an employee. Every driver who tries to compete in the Indy 500 has a story. The story revolves around the business deal they can put together. Sometimes these stories are short as the deal they put together never gets them the right car to drive or a car at all. Other times drivers get the right car, the right team, they win races, and, at the end of the deal, walk away on their own terms. But all who go down the road of trying to compete in the Greatest Spectacle in racing know that what they are getting into is a business deal. A business deal that will someday end as all business deals tend to come to a conclusion at some point or another—sometimes the way we like, other times not so.

LESSON LEARNED

All business revolves around the deals you will put together. You will not get some deals you feel you deserve. Other times you will get deals that surprise you and seem to come out of nowhere. You will learn that some deals are cancelled and it doesn't seem fair. I have learned that one should never take any deal for granted. When in a deal, you give it your all and deliver what you agreed to or more. When you do that, more and better deals will come your way, last longer and be of greater benefit to all involved. One should never take it personally when a business deal comes to an end. It simply means that one of the two parties feel that a change was needed. When it happens, take what you have learned, find a new deal, and win again.

PERSONAL STORY

I learned the hard way about the difference between employees, friends, and family. Up to 2008, I had created a staff that was fun to be around. I knew some of them were not the absolute best at what I had them doing, but they got the job done to a mostly acceptable level. Even though I had provided them with an excellent opportunity, I refrained from pushing them to be better and holding them accountable. I was under the illusion these people were my family and friends. I didn't want to hurt their feelings. I did not want them to quit. I knew they had families and financial responsibilities, and I wanted to help them as much as I could. The wake-up call came when the recession hit. My biggest business was tied directly to the automotive industry. I took a monster hit. Since my "friends and family"—employees—were my friends, I decided to take the personal financial hit so they would not have too. Boy was I dumb. I had to increase my hours by 20 a week to make things work—not my pay, just my hours. No problem. But when I asked "my friends and family" to help me out and put in a few more hours, make a few more calls, and help me do what was necessary to keep things going, all but three of them refused. The three that agreed to do more only would for more money. One, seeing how much I was working, knowing I was making a ton less so that they would even have a paycheck, had the gall to even ask for a raise. When I explained that it was not possible and pointed out all I was doing just to keep things going, she sarcastically replied that that was not her problem, she had put in five years and she wanted more! Wanted more amongst the worst financial crisis we had seen in over eighty years. It finally became as clear as day. These were not my friends and family. These were employees. This was a business deal. They saw it that way. I paid them to do something in a certain number of hours, they did it and went home.

It was new revelation. I immediately saw it as a business deal too. Yes, I could and should treat them like friends and family, but they were not. I put in new rules, new requirements and restructured the way they were paid. A new pay plan where they could actually make more, but they would have to earn it. As a matter of fact, if they wanted to make what they had before, they would have to earn it. No more passes, no more "good enough". Perform and get paid or don't and leave. Although three people left instantly—one was my biggest producer—business turned immediately and things got better instantly. The reason? I was running a business, and for the first time I was running it like a business. To this day, things have never been better. Now my policy is the same as being a driver in an Indy Car. Here is your seat. Here is what I need you to do while you are in the seat. As long as you can do that, you get to stay in the seat. The minute you cannot or will not do what that seat requires, you can no longer sit in it. It does not mean I like or dislike you. It does not mean we can't continue to be friends if it does not work out. It just means this is a business deal. It is about the team and the business. No one person is allowed to dictate how successful a team can be because they will not do what they are paid to do. Here is the best part about my new "it's a business deal" policy. My employees are happier, more productive, and earn more. I am more happy, my business continues to grow, and I make more money. It hurts me sometimes when I see a favorite driver of mine removed from their seat in the car. Unlike in the past when I did not understand, today I know it is simply a business deal. It is about the survival and growth of the team and not about just one individual. Trust me, it hurts every time it does not work out between me and an employee. There is a certain part of me that feels like I failed. I give every employee everything they need to be successful. I give them the opportunity to be successful. I will work with them and train them without regret. But sometimes tough decisions must be made that are best for the team and not necessarily the individual.

Points to Ponder

One of the biggest mistakes I see businesses make is that they believe that the people they hire to work for them are family and friends. Believing that, they allow their emotions to get in the way and keep people they should not keep who cannot do the job for far longer than they should. As you saw above, I have been guilty of this myself. When one person cannot or will not do his job, it affects all others in your company. You have to ask yourself, is it fair to allow one person to have that power and dictate how much earning and success you and your team will have? It's always been funny to me how we ignore, avoid, and pretty much disown real family members when we find they are not to our liking. In short, we fire them like employees. But employees who affect our success and livelihood we treat like favorite cousins and let them get away with theft and steal our careers.

CHAPTER 15
WINNER'S STEP AND THINK OUTSIDE THE BOX

1967 WITH ONLY FIVE LAPS to go, Parnelli Jones had the Indy 500 won. At that point he had lead nearly 171 laps with the car running in second being driven by A.J. Foyt, nearly a lap down and the car being driven by Al Unser Sr. in third place two laps down. It was Parnelli's day. From the very beginning of the race, on the opening lap, Parnelli, from his sixth starting position, swept around five cars on the outside before he got to turn two. That had never been done before or since. Shortly after coming off of turn two, he passed the leader and pole sitter, Mario Andretti, like Mario was just sitting still. It was obvious to all who witnessed this that Jones was going to show the world that although his one-of-a-kind Turbine engine car that omitted a "swish" instead of a roar may not be fast enough to get the pole position, but it had handling capabilities the likes the track had never seen before. So comfortable was Jones, that as he came down the front straightaway on that first lap way ahead of the other cars, he raised one hand off the steering wheel and gave the okay sign to his crew, as if to say, it will be our day!

The advantage that Parnelli had was in the car. Famous team owner Andy Granatelli had read the rules and discovered loopholes that would permit him to build such a car. Upon first view, all of the other drivers knew they would be in trouble come race day. The general feeling was that they would be driving for second place unless Jones had some bad luck in the race. He did. With his second Indy 500 fewer than eight miles away, coming off of turn four, a $6 transmission bearing failed and he coasted to the pit entrance and was credited with a sixth place finish.

Fast forward to 1994. Another famous team owner reads the rule book and finds a loophole and the BEAST is unleashed! Roger Penske and his team found a loophole that allowed them to secretly build an engine that would produce 1000 horsepower, giving it an immediate 150 to 200 horsepower advantage over every other engine in the field. They dominated the entire month. His drivers, two-time Indy 500 champion Emerson Fittipaldi, one- time Indy 500 champ Al Unser Jr., and the young Paul Tracey toyed with the other drivers all month long. Every practice day throughout the month of May they swapped places at the top of the speed charts. When it came time to qualify for the race, the only reason they did not sweep the top three spots is because earlier in the week, Paul Tracey had lost control of his beast and hit the wall, getting a concussion in the process. He was deemed not able to drive for a week, and he later qualified 25th on the second weekend of qualifications.

With Al Jr. on the pole, the race was no different. Little Al and Emmo dominated the race with Emmo leading a race high 145 laps and Little Al eventually leading 48. They dominantly led all but 7 laps of the race. These cars were untouchable. With about 15 laps to go, Fittipaldi had a two-lap lead over third place and was poised to pass his teammate Al Unser Jr., running in second, and put him a lap down. His second consecutive Indy 500 and third overall in hand, coming out of turn four, Emerson lost control of the car and smacked the turn four wall, giving Little Al his second Indy 500 victory. It was almost like the track was extracting revenge on Emerson from the year before when he won and refused to drink the traditional milk in the winner's circle. Delightfully letting him believe it was his race and taking it away in a most embarrassing way. All alone on the track, in the clear, no cars around, and like a rookie—BAM! Don't like milk? Now you won't have to drink it! If the track did not say that, the fans in the stands sure did as thousands jumped to their feet and cheered. The only time I have seen the crowd cheer when a driver crashed. They were the last laps Emerson ever drove in competition at the speedway. Can anyone say Karma?

But back to the point of the story. While many accused these teams of cheating and having an unfair advantage, I don't. I do admit that having watched the 1967 race several times on tape and being in the grandstands for the 1994 edition, these cars made it a little duller than most would like, but what an accomplishment. Indy always has been and always will be about being the best. Being the best in the car. Having the best team. Building the best machines AND knowing what the rules will not allow AND what the rules will allow. Both Roger Penske and Andy Granatellie did not look at the rule book and say, "What can't we do?" They looked at the rule book and asked, "What can we do?"

Lesson Learned

So many time's we get caught up in following the rules and staying within the "box" that the rules create that we forget that true invention and creativity comes many times by stepping outside the box and simply asking why not. I was so happy that month of May to see in real life, right in front of me, what happened when Mr. Penske taught me to step and think outside the box.

Personal Story

In 2007 on Super Bowl weekend, I was scheduled to speak at a major convention. When I accepted the speaking job nine months earlier, I did not realize it would be on the same day of the Super Bowl. It wasn't until the actual event got close that I realized my Indianapolis Colts may be actually playing in the game that year. When it was all said and done, the Colts would be playing the in Super Bowl for the first time as an Indianapolis team. Worse, my presentation was scheduled at the same time the game was set to start. I had waited since 1983 to see my team play in the Super Bowl, and now I would miss most of the first half. When I contacted the hosts of the event to see if there was any way I could switch with another speaker, the hosts responded with a big fat no! Show up as agreed or never work for them again. On top of that, I was told to not even mention the Super Bowl at any time during my presentation as they would be recording it and did not want my message dated with current events. They reminded me to read my contract which stated the same—no talking current events. Furthermore, many who were supposed to attend my presentation wanted to see the game too. This was a large convention with thousands of people in attendance. To make matters worse, at each speaking time throughout the day, there were always four speakers in different rooms making presentations at the same time. So, knowing that the number of people that would stay and listen verses cut for the game would be large, I had to figure out a way to get people in my room because, with the game, any speaker would be lucky to get a room 30% filled. This was a big event that would have a big impact on my earnings for the rest of the year. At conventions, if people see you speak and like what you say, they hire you. But they have to see you speak for that to happen, so I needed that room full.

Taking a page from Mr. Penske's book, I looked outside the box. My contract and the rules clearly stated that I was not allowed to TALK about current events, but it said nothing about being able to superimpose the score and information about the game on my presenter's screen that was being recorded internally and would not show on the recording. So, I let word get out the morning of the conference that attendees would be able to get info about the game during my presentation. It worked! My room was packed to standing room only.

I had my assistant rig a flashlight that she could shine in the upper right hand corner of my slides in order to announce important info, but mostly the score. It worked. Any time something big happened, from where she was sitting in the room, she would flash a small flashlight at me. When it was appropriate, I would say, "With that, let me show you something I think you will like." My assistant would then flash the updated score or info on the screen and the crowd would loudly applaud and cheer. Even though the hosts of the event did not like what I did, I had not broken any rules. In fact, I had delivered a recorded version that sounded highly exciting because of the cheering, making it one of the highest selling recordings in the event's history, plus the audience and I were able to stay up with the game, plus, because the way the recording sounded and from sheer audience appreciation for what I had done, I garnered 40% more business from the convention than I had projected. My thinking outside the box may have not gotten my face on the Indy 500 trophy, but I was able to keep my car off the wall and rule the day.

POINTS TO PONDER

Bobby Kennedy, presidential candidate and brother to President John F. Kennedy, said it best when he said, "There are those that look at things the way they are, and ask **why**? I dream of things that never were, and ask **why not**?" The only time I have found this question to not be good is at parties or during drinking contests.

CHAPTER 16
SOME DREAMS ARE JUST TOO BIG TO LET GO

In 1996, IndyCar Driver Buddy Lazier was in a practice crash in Phoenix Arizona and broke his back. His doctors told Buddy that he should not race for a year until his back completely healed. His doctors told him that his broken vertebrate looked like a smashed hard-boiled egg. There were 16 fractures and 25 bone fragments. He was told that if he drove and the car just wiggled or spun, let alone hit the wall, he would permanently injure his back and may never walk again. Having the best IndyCar to drive in his career, Buddy refused to sit out the Indy 500 that was to be run just under two months after his crash. Instead, he had a special seat made for the car. He was forced to sign a waiver from his insurance company stating that if he were to further injure his back, it would not be covered. Making it even more dangerous, when Buddy and the drivers got to Indy, the speeds were faster than they had ever been, before or since, just below the 240-mph mark. At speeds like that, it takes less to lose a car to a spin or crash than it does with the previous speeds in the 232 range. All month long, watching Buddy get in and out of his car during practice and qualifications made anyone who witnessed it cringe from Buddy's obvious pain. On race morning, when asked why he was taking such a great risk in one of the many interviews he did, Buddy said something along the lines of, "I have waited my whole Indy career to have a car and opportunity like this. To walk away for any reason and miss the opportunity would be to walk away as just another driver that drove the race. I want to prove that I have what it takes to race and win, and you just can't do that from the sidelines." Starting fifth that day, Buddy ran up front with the leaders the whole race, occasionally leading from time to time. He was showing the world that nothing could hold him back and that he did have what it takes. With just ten laps to go, Buddy found himself in third place. With eight to go he found himself in first place being chased down by second place driver Davey Jones after making a highly risky turn three pass on the high side of Jones. With just six laps to go, the caution flag was thrown because of a crash by Scott Sharp. As he had done all day long on the yellows, Buddy was extending his hands out of the cockpit and stretching in an effort to eliminate the extreme pain in his lower back. At that point, many felt the pain had overcome him. When the race returned to green with one lap to go, Lazier found himself driving hard into turn one in the lead, Jones not far off his tail. But by turn three, Lazier was several car lengths ahead and went on to win his first IndyCar race and the 80th running of the Indy 500. When Buddy got to the winner's circle, he could not lift himself out of the car due to the pain in his back. With help, he stood briefly so they could place the winner's wreath over his head and so that he could drink the Indy milk. The interview and winner's circle photos show a subdued driver with tears raining down his face—not from joy, but from the shear pain in his back. Buddy eventually healed and continues to drive to this day. After that race through 2001 he was a dominant force in IndyCar, winning seven more races at other tracks and winning the IndyCar championship in the year 2000.

LESSON LEARNED

One never knows what the conditions will be when you get your big break. Some dreams are just too big to let go. When your big break comes—and it will—will you pass it by because you view it as too risky and be an "also ran," or will you step up and show the world what you are made of?

PERSONAL STORY

Growing up, I knew my dad was a very hard worker. A truck driver that delivered liquor to liquor stores, bars, restaurants, and grocery stores, he was typically out of the house by 5:30 am, not to return most nights until 7:00 or 8:00 pm. I remember times as a child seeing him leave for work with a hole in his shoe so his kids would not have to. There were days when he left with no lunch or no lunch money so his kids would have lunch money at school. He never complained and never felt sorry for the situation he many times found himself in due to the many illnesses his wife and kids had. He never felt sorry for himself when the company he had driven for for twenty-nine and half years filed for bankruptcy because the owner's alcoholic son had taken over the business and drank it into insolvency, taking my dad's pension with it just six months before my dad was to retire and leaving both him and my mom nearly destitute. The only regret he ever shared with me was that at two different times he was offered opportunities to better himself. Once he was offered the chance to become an over the road semi-truck driver with a friend by starting a small trucking firm and using trucks that they would need to take loans out to secure. Another time he was offered the opportunity to work with my uncle who owned a grocery store and invest in the butcher part of the business. In both cases, he turned down the opportunities because in one instance my mom was pregnant and in the other he would have had to mortgage his house to get involved. He feared what may happen if things didn't work out. Had he done either, my dad's life, at least financially, would have been many times easier since both of those situations paid off handsomely for the people who stepped in when my dad felt he could not. My dad only discussed these with me on three different occasions. Every time he did, I saw the deep regret in his eyes. I asked him about that regret once, and he said, "The regret I have is not about what 'I' could have had, but what I could have provided for you kids and your mother. You should live your life with no regrets." I had seen what living with regret could look and feel like. I wanted no part of it, and you should not either.

Buddy Lazier must have seen what regret could do to another as well and wanted no part of it. He had no fear in his life and was not about to allow regret to be a part of it either.

POINTS TO PONDER

Noted 20th century author Fulton Oursler said it best when he said, "Many of us crucify ourselves between two thieves—regret for the past and fear of the future." I only have one regret in my life. Once at the end of a first date with a girl I was crazy about and who seemed to be crazy about me, she invited me in for a nightcap. Right before disappearing into her bedroom to get into something more comfortable, with a wink, she instructed me to quickly return to my car and pick out a fun cassette tape to play on her stereo from the vast collection I had shown her that I had in my car. I selected the newly released "Kiss Alive II" double album and put it on. I really regret that.

I guess in the end, the idea is to live life with no bigger regrets than wishing you had selected the fried calamari as your appetizer instead of the edamame.

CHAPTER 17
CHANGE OR BE LEFT BEHIND

GARY BETTENHAUSEN WAS PART OF the legendary fan favorite Bettenhausen racing family. Gary Bettenhausen's dad, Tony Sr., famously raced in 12 Indy 500s from 1946 through 1960, dying in a crash at the famed speedway in 1961 while testing a car for that year's race. Gary, the first of three racing sons of Tony's, was an instant fan favorite when he first came to Indy. He was a winner on smaller tracks and immediately fast at Indy in his first four starts there. So fast in fact, that in 1972 he caught the eye of a young Roger Penske and was selected to drive for him that year. It looked like a great choice as Gary led the 1972 Indy 500 for 138 laps before his car failed and he finished 14th. His teammate, Mark Donahue, won the race that day. Clearly, Gary was driving on a team that had fast cars and could win at Indy. It was apparent to everyone that if you drove for Penske racing, you had a shot to not only win at Indy, but on any race track. Problem was, Penske drivers were not allowed to drive Midget, Sprint, Silver Crown cars or any type of car that raced on dirt tracks. Gary refused to agree to that. After all, that is where his family had made their name, on the small dirt tracks in the Midwest. So, in 1974, while driving a Silver Crown car on dirt in New York, Gary was in a horrible crash that left his left arm permanently paralyzed. Although he continued to drive race cars until 1996, in 1974 Penske let him go, and he never had another great car to drive at Indy. Looking back over his career after retiring from racing, Gary said it was the biggest regret and mistake in life that he refused to change and do what Roger asked. Where Roger had seen the role of race car drivers changing from that of a "jack of all trades" to more of a specialist in a single discipline, Gary hung onto the past and was left in the past. Had Gary simply accepted change and continued to drive for Roger, one can only imagine what may have happened since Penske's teams won the Indy 500 nine more times between 1974 when Gary was fired to 1996 when he retired.

LESSON LEARNED

Effectively manage change. Expect change. Embrace change. Create change. Change is good. Change is growth. Change is inevitable. You cannot stop it and you cannot slow it down. If you fight change, you will be left behind and ultimately replaced to make room for the individual who can adapt. Having the ability to be flexible and effectively manage change means you have the skills to survive.

Personal Story

The importance of change in sales, business, and life has always been easy for me. By simply watching what was going on around me, I found it very apparent early on the value in being open to and actually being able to change. Stories Like Gary Bettenhausen's seemed to be everywhere. Look at music for instance. The average band lasts for three maybe four albums. Why? Because they put albums out that all sound the same while their fans grow and change. One of the things that made the band the Beatles so big and popular was its ability to change and grow with its audience. If you compare their first album with the last, it sounds almost like two completely different bands. Whether they did it consciously or not, I do not know. But by doing it, they secured a legacy like no other band has before or since. When people refuse or are unable to change, they are forced to go away. At this writing, we are watching a company that is one hundred plus years old go out of business because it refuses to change. The Yellow Cab company and taxi cab companies in general will likely be all but gone within the next five years. Why? Because instead investing a few hundred thousand dollars in a mobile app like Uber and Lyft have done and taking those two companies on, they seemingly believe that people like me are someday going to prefer to go back to the past. They believe that I will land one day in the future in an airport like Chicago O'Hare in the middle of January when it is five degrees outside, collect my luggage from baggage claim, go outside in the harsh cold, and stand in line for thirty to forty minutes with fifty other people and wait for a cab to pull up. A cab that will most likely be dirty with a bullet proof plastic divider that screams NOT SAFE and that has been poorly maintained. They are convinced I will want to go back to that instead of just merely collecting my bags, and, while standing in a climate controlled building, open an app and select a car that I can watch approach on my phone. A car that has a driver that will call and/or text me just prior to their arrival so I can walk out to meet them where they will put my bags in their car for me, open my door where I will enter a clean, well-maintained vehicle and ride with a friendly driver that will offer me a bottle of water. Later, upon arriving to my destination, they will again open my door and hand me my bags, and I will simply walk away without an awkward exchange of cash or credit cards since the app will collect my fare with tip if I chose to give one. Yellow Cab and other cab companies are convinced that I will leave that and go back to the past. Sure. They will change eventually. Change from a company that existed for over one-hundred years to one that becomes a footnote in history.

POINTS TO PONDER

One of America's most quoted writers, William Arthur Ward, said it best when he said, "The pessimist complains about the wind; the optimist expects it to change; the realist adjusts the sails." In business, it is probably time for a change of some type if your boss or your client ask you out for dinner and they refer to it as "The Last Supper."

CHAPTER 18
"I WASN'T GOING TO FINISH SECOND"

1998 INDY 500 CHAMPION EDDIE Cheever won the race by driving the best race of his life. Up to that point in his career, he had driven in well over 200 major open wheel races in both IndyCar and Formula One. It was obvious from the start of the 1998 IndyCar season that Cheever was on a mission. Now the owner of his own IndyCar team and in the twilight of his racing career, Eddie was driving, again, like a man motivated. On the very first turn of the very first lap of the 1998 Indy 500, starting from 17th position, Eddie was bumped from behind and slid sideways for more than two hundred yards toward turn two. The crowd of several hundred thousand jumped to their feet believing they were seeing the end of Eddie's race day. Somehow, Eddie was able to regain control of the car—he was motivated. Flat spotting his tires, he was forced into the pits for fresh tires, moving him to the back of the field. When the race restarted, Eddie drove a fast and calculated race, eventually making his way to the front and trading the lead of the race with other front runners while managing to lead 76 laps! He was motivated. Cheever experienced five more close calls during the race. None his fault, but close calls nonetheless. It seemed he was not only expected to race the other 32 drivers, but Lady Luck herself. But it was the final six laps that astounded the thousands in the stands and the millions watching on television. After a crash on the track, the race was restarted with six laps to go. Cheever was in front with 1996 Indy 500 champion Buddy Lazier fewer than two car lengths back. Coming up to speed, Cheever wove back and forth on the track to keep Buddy behind him. As Cheever came off of turn two, he came within inches of the wall. Same thing off of turns three and four and every turn after that. He was motivated. Eddie was using every inch of the track and driving his race car on a race line never seen before. This was a highly dangerous way to drive. No one had done it before. Even the announcers were stunned at what they were seeing. It was not clear if Eddie was so fast he was pulling away from the cars behind or if they were backing up just a bit waiting for him to lose control and crash so they could take the lead. It was a stunning show of determination, grit, and bravery. The crowd loved it each time Eddie exited a corner, literally just inches away from the wall. So close, that legend has it, that the wall itself would close its eyes and hold its breath each time he went through a corner. It was thrilling to watch. Eddie went on to win by a wide margin, becoming the first owner driver to win the Indy 500 since AJ Foyt had done it in 1977. In the winner's circle, Eddie was asked why he was driving so close to the wall. His reply, "I wasn't going to finish second." His motivation was clear as day. When asked what Indy meant, his reply was that his father had told him when he started his racing career, that if he was to win only one race, it should be the Indy 500, so Eddie dedicated the win to his father. But there was second motivation on that day. It was to prove his ex-girlfriend wrong. When asked in the winner's circle if he was going to be celebrating later with his girlfriend, he replied, "I'm afraid not. She dumped me last night because she said I would never amount to anything. I will be celebrating for sure, but not with her."

LESSON LEARNED

Motivation can come from many places for many reasons. Whether that motivation comes for the love another or in spite of another, it is how you channel it that will make the difference. I have always believed, as I can only assume Eddie Cheever did, that you must draw from what is burning inside you, good or bad, and use it to motivate yourself to achieve only good. Even though part of Eddie's motivation that day stemmed from a bad situation, he did not allow it to bring him down, but instead he delivered good.

PERSONAL STORY

"You are now going to hell and will be broke once you get there!" Spoken by an ex-girlfriend that had selected the college she would attend based on where I was going upon learning that I had changed my mind about higher education and was foregoing my college career for a career in professional shoe sales at the mall.

"You don't know shit, you do not have any shit, and you

will never amount to shit!" Spoken by my ex-wife right before she told me she was filing for divorce and walked out the door.

"Why I would I go out with a loser like Jeff Cowan? He is only 20 years old and has already been married and divorced. There has to be something wrong with him." Spoken to my best friend by the first girl I had the hots for and wanted to go out with after my divorce.

"I think the girls in your past are all idiots and I will support you in whatever you want to do until my dying breath. I think you are the best man to ever walk the planet and can and will be whatever you want to be." Spoken by the love of my life, Mrs. Candy Cowan.

I believe I fully understand what motivated Eddie Cheever in 1998 as he won the Indy 500. Every one of those comments have and continue to motivate me every day I get out of bed to prove the women from past wrong and to prove my very dedicated wife right.

Points to Ponder

What Eddie taught me is that motivation need not come all from bad situations, it can and should come for the good as well. I have learned the hard way that motivation derived solely from hate or anger can get you what you want, but it will have a bitter taste more times than not. Your motivation has to be equally gained from the desire to be and do good for others as well as yourself for the end result to be truly satisfying. It took me 18 years to discover those women from my early days were right, but by that time I had met Candy and discovered she was right too. Mae West was right when she said; "Too much of a good thing can be wonderful."

CHAPTER 19
A LOT OF KNOWLEDGE, A LITTLE TEAM AND A BIG WIN

FAN FAVORITE TONY KANAAN BECAME a fan favorite for his tenacious driving, winning spirit, and humble attitude. Kanaan hit the Indy 500 running hard. He is the first and only driver to lead the race in his first seven starts. In 2004, he finished every single lap in every race on the IndyCar Circuit—the only driver to ever do so in any major driving series—and he won the series championship that same year. During that same season he led 889 laps—a record. In 2010 he became only the second driver to start the race in 33rd position and lead a lap. By that time, he had won 14 other IndyCar races. With all of those accomplishments driving for the famous Andretti racing team for eight years, his contract was cancelled at the end 2010 when his longtime sponsor, Seven-Eleven, announced they would not be renewing their sponsorship of Tony. He could lead at Indy, but he seemingly could not win it. Much to our dismay as fans, we were all reminded that racing is a business first and entertainment second. There is a lot at stake in racing. Sponsors pay the teams and drivers big money to put their name on the side of cars. They do it because they want to win and win big. It's a business deal. Tony was not the first driver to have this happen, and he will not be the last. More times than not when this happens in Indy Racing, the drivers seem to just fade away. They may drive here or there for a few more years, but most never recover. Tony was different. With all of the top rides taken and no other big teams calling, Kanaan signed with the small, winless racing team, KV racing, owned by one of his friends and a former driver, Jimmy Vasser.

Having seen many drivers start their climb down the ladder in the past, many thought this was Tony's first step toward being out of IndyCar and being remembered as just another driver that was *the* fan favorite, but a favorite who never won. Everyone thought that, except for Tony Kanaan that is. Tony knew he had one thing that many drivers before him and even many of his contemporaries did not have—knowledge. Knowledge of how to win races, knowledge of how to make a car go fast, knowledge of how to motivate those around him with his contagious smile and outlook on life. And most importantly, knowledge of knowing how to lead at the Indy 500.

Even with all of his knowledge, Tony was not able to help much the first two years with his new team. The first year, the team had made a poor engine choice that had a serious lack of horsepower. The second year saw improvements, but it was his third year in 2013 that his knowledge paid off. Arguably, the toughest Indy 500 ever contended, it was clear from the start that no rookie was going to win this race. This was a race that was going to be won by a veteran who knew the track and knew it well. Tony had the drive of his lifetime that day. Battling everything that one could in a race. Being near the front of the field and leading the race several times throughout the day, what he had to contend with had never been seen before and has not since. Here is what happened that day:

The race ended being the fastest ever run (187.433 including caution laps) with the fewest number of caution laps ever (21) with a record number of 133 consecutive laps ran without a caution. Kanaan was among a record 14 drivers that swapped the lead fiercely amongst themselves throughout the day for a record 68 times. It seemed nearly everyone driving that day was invincible as a record 26 drivers were still racing at the conclusion of the race.

With just four laps to go, the race was restarted after a crash and found Tony screaming down the main straight in second place just behind Ryan Hunter-Reay with Carlos Munoz inches behind him. In a sweeping, thrilling move, the three cars fanned out and became three wide as they approach turn one. Inches apart, Kanaan darts to the inside line and barely edges out the other two for the lead. The crowd went insane as *the* fan favorite and most beloved driver drove into the short chute between turns one and two, pulling ahead with a slight advantage. Diving into turn two and coming out the other side, Kanaan saw the yellow lights flash on, indicating the caution flag was being waved. Dario Franchitti had smacked the wall on the restart heading into turn one. In the process, he had ensured that Tony Kanaan would be added to the list of Indy 500 champions. Realizing this, the gigantic crowd of thousands went into near hysterics like I have never seen before or since.

Tony Kanaan had prepared himself for this very race his entire life. In his off time, he competes in the Ironman Triathlon and is one of the most physically fit drivers to ever drive an IndyCar. Because of this, he had the stamina needed for a race with so few caution laps, so much non-stop action and passing every lap. The Ironman Triathlon taught him how to maintain focus and have clear thought under the toughest of circumstances. He used that knowledge to his advantage. He had been in every situation that he was forced to face that day. That past knowledge served him well as he proved he knew how to handle it all. His knowledge that he shared with his teammates made a difference and helped them get their first ever win of any type that day. He pulled from that vast library of knowledge that day and outsmarted, out preformed, and simply out drove every other driver in the field. When nearly everyone else was ready to give up on Tony, he knew he had the one thing so few others had. He had knowledge, and he sold that knowledge to a small team that believed in him. Tony pulled from that knowledge and completed his long-life goal—he won the Indy 500. The toughest one ever run before or since. He not only won it for himself, but for a smaller team who recognized his knowledge and used it to win the biggest race in the world.

LESSON LEARNED

All throughout your career you must study and prepare for every possible situation you may find yourself in, even when that training and preparation seems like it is for the unlikeliest of situations. You never know when the knowledge you gain from that time training and preparing will be needed and give you that slight edge you need to win. The Indy 500 has taught me this over and over throughout the years. All one needs to do is walk through the garage area of Indianapolis to see the many past drivers that have been hired as consultants for their knowledge so that they can share it and make a difference for the young and inexperienced.

PERSONAL STORY

I read one time that according to the National Library Association, if you were to read just one book a month for 12 months you would be in the top 25% of all intellectuals in the world. Furthermore, if you were to read just five books on any subject, you would be one of the world's foremost authorities on that subject. It also reported that, based on the average reading speed of people and based on the average length of a book today, that if you could read for just 15 minutes a day you would be able to complete 20 books in a year. Curious to see how true this was, I did some research. Here is what I found: 26th U.S. President Teddy Roosevelt would read a book before breakfast every day, and depending on his schedule, another two or three in the evening. Investor and billionaire Warren Buffett reads five hundred pages and five different newspapers a day. Microsoft founder Bill Gates reads fifty books a year. Mark Zuckerberg, who invented Facebook, reads a book every two weeks. Mark Cuban, Dallas Mavericks Basketball team owner and entrepreneur, reads three hours every day. Elon Musk, who co-founded PayPal and Tesla Auto, has been known to read up to ten hours a day. 43rd U.S. President George Bush has been known to read as many as two books a week reading a high of 95 books in the year of 2006.

Since leaving office, he has slowed his pace to about 50 a year or one a week.

In nearly every major business deal I have closed, I can say I did it by having more knowledge on the subject at hand verses my competition. Even when I was working for various companies in my early selling career, I always made it a point to know not only my product inside and out, but my competitions' as well. I also find it necessary to stay up on current affairs in the various towns I am visiting. Whenever possible, I make it my job to find out as much as I can about who I am presenting my products to. In short, just like Tony Kanaan and all of the highly successful people I have mentioned here, knowledge gives you power. You can lose your job and everything you have, but if you have knowledge, no one can ever take that away from you. The more knowledge you have, the more valuable you are to those around you. I cannot state for fact that KV Racing hired Tony Kanaan only for his knowledge of driving IndyCars, but I would be willing to bet it was their biggest motivating factor. You may be able to take the driver out of the car, but you can't take the knowledge away from the driver who gained it when driving.

Points to Ponder

Want to be the best salesperson in your business? Step one, become a product expert in your field. That will get you in the top 50% of any sales team for any given product. Step two, to get to the top 20%, where typically the best, highest paid and most secure professionals reside, in addition to being a product expert, you have to master the skills of selling. The way you accomplish that is to read two "How To" selling books to every one product book you read when you first start. Once you have mastered your product, read at least two books a year regarding your product and six regarding selling. Your product may become obsolete at any given moment, meaning it can be taken away and your knowledge of it becomes worthless. The knowledge you gain about selling can never be taken away. The knowledge of selling you possess will determine your value and the level of security you enjoy. As Benjamin Franklin once said, "An investment in knowledge always pays the best interest."

CHAPTER 20
SOMETHING TO LIVE FOR

THE 1986 INDY 500 I remember vividly for a number of reasons. First, a heavy rain soaked us all and the race was rescheduled for the next day and then rescheduled again for the following Saturday as the weather was bad all week. Second, when the race was run, it was the closest three-car finish up to that time and came right down to the wire. Third, I learned that having a purpose in life can actually extend your life.

When the 1986 race finally started, you could tell it was going to be a fast one. Michael Andretti jumped out in the lead and held it for the first 42 laps, but it was near the middle of the race when things heated up. Three cars basically shot to the front and dueled with each other for the remainder of the race. Bobby Rahal, Kevin Cogan, and Rick Mears. With just 14 laps to go, Rick Mears was in the lead with Bobby Rahal right on his tail and Cogan on Rahal's. Coming up on a lapped rookie driver on the backstretch, Rahal drove under Mears and took the lead. By the time they reached the front stretch, Cogan had enough to pass Mears. Now in second, Cogan found himself side by side with Rahal. Cogan took the low side underneath another lapped car and Rahal fanned out to take the high side around. In doing so, Cogan had the edge and took the lead. For the next eight laps, Cogan drove like a man possessed. Getting so close to the walls on the exits of each corner, he nearly crashed several times while extending his lead to over just three seconds. With just five laps to go, Arie Luyendyk spun coming off of turn four, bringing out the caution flag and instantly washing away the wide lead Cogan had created with his frantic driving. On the restart with two laps to go, Cogan came off of four in the lead but lost it as Rahal jumped to the inside line and raced him side by side toward turn one before pulling away. Over the next two laps, Rahal posted two of the fastest laps of the race and won the race with Cogan and Mears just over one second back, making it the closest three car finish in the Indy 500s history. On the last lap, the fastest lap ever completed in competition, up to that time, was posted by Rahal at 209 plus mph. Also, during the last lap, Rahal's fuel light was flashing, indicating he was about to run out of fuel. It was also the first time the race had been run in less than three hours. It was a highly dramatic race with a dramatic finish that made it an instant classic. Since being run, it has become one of the most popular episodes played on ESPN Classic.

But it was in the winner's circle where things got real for me and the many thousands at the race that day. Bobby Rahal was a very subdued winner. Fighting back tears, he took a small, quick sip of Budweiser beer, his sponsor, and then a small, quick sip of the famous milk. When asked by ABC pit reporter, Jack Arute, in the winner's circle why he was so subdued, Bobby simply replied, "I'm almost in tears. This one is for Jim Trueman. . . . If there is one thing I can give Jim Trueman it is this. . . . he is the highest quality human being and I knew my great days would come with him." With that, the crowd became quieted and many started crying themselves. He reminded us that team owner Jim Trueman had cancer and was in the latest stages of that cruel diseases grasp. Many thought it was a miracle he was even at the track. When Jim showed up in the winner's circle next to his champion driver, Bobby handed him the milk. Jim took a long drink of the milk and then said, "It could not have been better!"

Mr. Trueman was a businessman who owned 155 Red Roof Inn hotels. He was a racer himself. He began driving in 1962 and drove the Can-Am series through the 1970's, winning 125 races in 23 years. In addition, he was the SCCA national champion in the years 1975 and 1978. He was the first to give Bobby Rahal a professional race car to drive, and the Indy 500 was always the goal. In 1985, his third year at the track as a team owner, Jim learned he had cancer. He kept it quiet, and when he showed up at the speedway in 1986, he was visibly frail and quiet. He had what I believed to be a purpose, and that purpose was to win the Indy 500. Just like some wish to see a daughter walk down the aisle or see a child graduate from school when they know their time is limited, Jim's purpose was the Indy 500. One might imagine that he asked the "Powers that Be" to make the month last as long as possible. Maybe that is why it rained and added another week to the month? Who knows? I imagine this because after the interview was over in the winner's circle that day, Jim Trueman whispered in the ear of pit reporter, Jack Arute, "I can go now." Eleven days later, his purpose realized, Indy 500 Champion Team Owner Jim Trueman succumbed to cancer.

Lesson Learned

I have had many highly successful people tell me that once they reach their family, business, and financial goals, they then turn their energy toward a higher purpose. It is this purpose that drives them on, keeps them alive, and rewards them with a more meaningful life. Where a goal usually has a finite time put to it, a purpose gives one a reason to keep on keeping on. It may be as simple as getting the grandkids off the bus and watching them until their parents get home. It may be to give your time to a charity, church, or school. As has been proven in hundreds of studies, a purpose gives a person a reason to live and can and actually does prolong one's life.

Personal Story

I can't say that I have ever met person who loved another like my dad did my mom. That man was absolutely crazy about my mom. She was his purpose. He told me countless times that he was there to take care of "mother," his term of endearment regarding my mom. From the time he had his first heart attack at the age of 42, he willed himself back to health so that he could make sure that she would be alright. For another thirty plus years, he battled several more heart attacks, cardiovascular disease, and losing a leg at the knee from acute diabetes. He always fought back, was always employed, was always working so that my mom would be safe. He told me many times that he had promised her that he would love her and take care of her until the end, and he did. It was only after he became wheelchair bound the last years in his life that I noticed him starting to change. My mom, whose love was as equal to his as possible, went above and beyond to make sure he had everything he needed. Although my dad was able to do most things for himself, when it came time to go anywhere in a car, my mom would have to lift his heavy wheelchair in and out of the trunk of their Buick. After doing so for a number of years, my mom damaged her shoulder to the extent of needing surgery. It affected my dad in a big way. He started seeing himself as burden to her, and his health started to wane. One morning in December of 2011, my dad had a mild heart attack. After years of medical miracles, the doctors told him that they could do a procedure that would save his life and add up to another five years to his life. The bad news was that there was a better than 50% chance that he would end up a bedridden invalid for the remainder of his life. If he chose not to do the procedure, he would live only another two weeks. He chose not to have the procedure done. Heartbroken, I tried my damndest to convince him otherwise. It was when he looked at me and said, "I will not take the chance and become a burden to your mother. I always have said that when the day comes that I can no longer take care of her, I become a burden. I will not become a burden and make her life any more difficult than necessary." He had lost his purpose and on January 12th, 2012, at the age of 79, he passed.

Points to Ponder

Having a purpose in life gives you life. It gives you a longer and happier life. Comedian Jim Carrey said it best when he said, "I think everybody should get rich and famous and do everything they ever dreamed of so they can see that it's not the answer." Everyone must identify their own purpose. When I was young, I thought my purpose was to work hard and make my parents' lives easier. As I grew, I felt my purpose change to making sure those who worked for me had the lives they deserved. My purpose changed again when I married my wife Candy, as I felt it was my purpose to make her life as easy and secure as possible. It changed further when my grandkids came about. Looking back over my life to this point, I have uncovered what I believe my true purpose is. It is to do to all of those things and serve God. It is not the goals you reach that will make your life meaningful. It is the purpose you serve that will.

CHAPTER 21
SETTING YOURSELF ON FIRE

I WALKED INTO THE INDIANAPOLIS Motor Speedway gift shop one day to buy some postcards. I buy them to send to customers as a way to stand out or at least be different. There have been some great postcards over the years. For years, the Speedway used to sell one that had Emerson Fittipaldi sitting in his 1989 winning car at the start finish line with the Borg Warner Trophy and one million dollars stacked around him, as he was the first driver to win one million dollars for winning the race. It always got prospects and clients to call back. A postcard with the start of the race on the front is always a winner too. But the day I walked in a saw the postcard with a picture of Bill Simpson sitting in a chair on fire from head to toe in the first turn was one I won't forget anytime soon. That postcard became the most popular one I ever sent out.

So why was Simpson on fire? Bill Simpson was a race car driver and safety equipment manufacturer for race car drivers of all walks. Knowing that fire was and is the biggest threat and fear for drivers everywhere, Simpson developed what was truly the first fully fireproof race suit. The problem was, no one believed that it really worked. After being heckled by many in the garage area, Bill Simpson sent a letter to all the teams, sponsors, track personnel, and other race suit suppliers. In the letter, he challenged the other suppliers to sit side by side with him and light themselves on fire to test the suit and see whose suit was actually the best. He invited everyone else that wanted to watch to come and see the spectacle. Although no other suppliers showed, a whole bunch of track personnel and drivers did. At the stated time, Bill, wearing one of his suits, poured gasoline on himself from head to toe and lit himself on fire. As the shocked spectators, reportedly including several drivers like A.J. Foyt, Mario Andretti, and Johnny Rutherford, watched, Simpson made his point. He proved that if in a fiery crash while wearing one of his suits, you could not only survive, but survive without being burnt or disfigured.

Although the postcard was close cropped picture of the event, if you ever get the opportunity to visit the Indy photo shop on the second floor of the Indianapolis Motor Speedway Museum, there is a wide angle shot showing Johnny Rutherford standing next to Simpson with a stick that has two hot dogs attached to it. Rutherford was actually roasting hot dogs from the flames that had engulfed Bill's body while the others stood and laughed for the 50 or 60 seconds he was on fire. Here is the best part: they may have been clowning around at the presentation, but the next morning it was the talk of Gasoline Alley at the speedway. In the 1970 Indy 500, the year this happened, Simpson outfitted 30 of the 33 drivers in the field. Simpson safety equipment became and is still seen today as the leader in safety equipment for race car drivers everywhere.

LESSON LEARNED

You can have the best product on the planet, but if people cannot touch, see, feel, smell, hear, or experience it themselves, it may all be for naught. You have to be willing to put it all on the line and do whatever it takes, within the limits of the law, to prove you have what is the best if you really want others to believe it enough to give you money for it.

PERSONAL STORY

My first business that I started was a pure sales training business. I figured since every company that I had worked for had me get involved with training new recruits that it must be my calling. I had proven with every company that I had worked with that I could sell and sell well. I also had proven that I had the ability to not only train others, but I also had the ability to motivate them to be the absolute best they could be. Knowing that, I opened my own sales training company. Problem was, there are a lot of people out there that are convinced that they are great salespeople, great trainers, and great motivators. In reality, many are, so they, too, started their own companies. I had to make myself stand out, so I took a page out of Bill Simpsons playbook and begin demonstrating my ability. I became known and am still known to this day as the trainer who can not only train others to sell and motivate them, but as someone who will walk the walk and actually do what I teach. Countless times I have gone into businesses, done a quick study on their products and then presented those products to real prospects and closed deals. Clothing, shoes, furniture, automotive service, vehicle sales, widgets of all kinds, software, etc. My product is that I will not only train you, but after doing so, will stand side by side with you as you work with your customers, coaching, critiquing, and actually presenting your product if needed to show that I can not only train it, I can do it, proving in the process that my content and training works. Today I have a whole team of trainers that do the same. I have built a very successful business from this model. The way I saw it, if a guy like Bill Simpson was willing to set himself on fire to show how much he believed in his product, then simply talking to a business's customers and showing my products did what I said they would was easy. Thank you Mr. Simpson! You not only kept the drivers I love to watch safe, but you gave me a business model that has proven to be priceless.

POINTS TO PONDER

If you want your customers to buy your product, show them in the biggest way possible why it is the greatest. Do what Bill Simpson did. Be a showman. The same principle applies when you are a team leader. If you want to be the best sales manager or business owner you can be, show your team how much you believe in what you are asking them to do by doing it yourself. So many times I see successful people move up the ladder to the big comfy chair, and then they never want to get out of it. If you want your customers to buy your product, show them in the biggest way possible why it is the greatest. If you want your team to believe you are the greatest, get out of that big comfy chair and show your team why you got there in the first place. Many can talk the talk, but the truly successful motivate those around them by being willing to publicly walk the talk. Be a showman when presenting your products to your customers and be a showman when leading your team.

"Fortune always favors the brave, and never helps a man who does not help himself."

—P.T. BARNUM

CHAPTER 22

BE CAREFUL WHAT YOU ASK FOR

IN 1995, AT THE START of the race, I had my racing radio headset on and the volume up as loud as it would go. Racing radios and headsets allow you to hear the drivers talk to their teams as they race. They also allow you to hear an unfiltered television broadcast and the safety teams that help the drivers in the event of trouble on the track. As the cars came of off turn four for the start of the race in what was supposed to be a formation of eleven rows of three, it looked like only the first row was aligned correctly from our vantage point in the first turn. I listened as TV broadcaster Paul Page confirmed what we were seeing as the mis-aligned field came to the green flag at the start finish line. Always the best part of the race, the cars seemed to be a little faster than normal and the middle of the field was definitely out of whack as they got closer. With 350,000 spectators watching on, it took just seconds for the cars to reach us in turn one as everyone held their collective breath.

Turn one on the opening lap is always the most dangerous part of the race. Adrenaline pumping through the drivers' veins faster than an Indiana tornado, their heart rates soaring, focus and dependence on the skill of the drivers around them on the track is all that concerns them at this point. All know that the race is won on the last lap and not the first. Step one is to survive the first corner and the opening lap. But in 1995, it was not meant to be. In the blink of an eye eight-time Indy 500 starter, Stan Fox, went low in the first turn, hit the rumble strips, and spun toward the wall, taking future Indy 500 Champion Eddie Cheever with him. As the two hit the wall, Fox's car hit so hard that the nose of the car was ripped off completely, leaving his full body exposed. Still strapped to the seat and the back of the car, he went up on the back of Cheever's car and landed hard, up right on the track. By the time the accident was over, Stan was sitting on the track, fully exposed, still strapped to the back of the car, motionless. The crowd went silent. Many, in shock from what they had seen, had tears spilling from their eyes. Some left their seats and never returned. All prayed that Stan, the workingman's driver, as he was known, would be all right. Still unconscious, he was put in the ambulance. He miraculously lived and recovered after a long stay in the hospital, but after eight tries at Indy, he never raced again. The working man's racer was later inducted into the National Midget Auto Racing Hall of Fame for the immense amount of success he had had in that form of racing.

I was at the track on a practice day in 1990 and saw when driver Jim Crawford spun on the track coming into turn one and launched his car 15 feet into the air.

I was there in 1991 standing in the stands at the entrance to pit road on fast Friday, the day before qualifications where drivers try to squeeze everything out their cars possible. The lap before, I had told my friend, "Watch Dismore. He has an odd line heading into four. Let's hope he backs down a little." Less than 40 seconds later, he had one of the most spectacular crashes anyone has ever survived, hitting the turn four wall and bouncing across the track, hitting the inside wall so hard that he actually put a hole in the wall. He kept sliding hitting the pit wall, destroying his car as it shattered into hundreds of pieces. He survived and raced again, but not before a long stay in the hospital.

I was at Fontana when Gregg Moore had his crash. In Vegas when Dan Wheldon had his. I watched in the 101st running of the Indy 500 on about lap 35 when Jay Howard hit the turn one wall, careened across the track, and collected driver Scott Dixon, and I watched the cars literally fly end over end twenty feet up in the air. Every time I witness one of these crashes, my heart drops, my gut hurts, and I freeze until I see that the drivers are safe. Sadly, sometimes they are not.

I have seen more than my fair share of crashes over the years, and I truly pray before each race that I never see another one. If you have never seen one, you don't want to. I say that because I have taken hundreds of people to the Indianapolis Motor Speedway over the years and to many other tracks where the IndyCars have raced. I have been a tour guide on several occasions in an effort to help friends with suites and show their clients around. In doing so, so many times first timers will make the comment, "Boy, if there is a crash, I hope it happens right in front of us." I am not being judgmental—I myself said the same thing when I saw my first race. I repeated it too, right up to the time I saw a big one right in front of me. Luckily today, the cars are safer, and it is astonishing how many of these modern-day crashes have drivers simply get out of their cars after a crash, get in a backup car, and drive again. The cars have gotten so safe to drive that we forget sometimes that the drivers are real people with real families and real lives. Every once in a while, we are sadly reminded of those facts when someone does get hurt or worse. I think nearly all people who attend a race for the first time want to see a crash. I know I did. But real race fans don't. They know that life typically will deliver what you ask for, so they ask just to see a really great race that is safe for all involved.

LESSON LEARNED

Be careful what you ask for because you just might get it. I have learned that whether it be a business deal or a life matter, if I ask for something and work toward it, it is more likely that I will get it than not. IndyCar taught me that before I even make a comment about something I want or think I want, I do my research into just what I am asking for. If I discover that what I think I might want is actually something that I do indeed want, then and only then do I ask for it.

PERSONAL STORY

I was in grade seven when my dad had his first heart attack at the age of 42. The heart attack was so bad that mom was told when she first got to the hospital to prepare her goodbyes and tell dad anything she wanted him to know because it was going to be a rough fight and dad may not make it. This was all happening at a time in the early seventies when all young boys were fighting with their parents to have long hair. I had finally won the argument with my parents and had gotten my hair to a length that finally covered my ears and covered the collar on my shirt. I was fighting for shoulder length hair and only dreamed about ponytail length hair like the really cool guys and rock stars had. My dad hated all of the hair stuff. He was a decorated war veteran that fought with valor in the Korean War. Upon returning home with the war over, the U.S. Army made him a drill instructor for new recruits. My dad wore a flattop shaved head until he reached his 60's. He hated long hair on boys. Not considering the consequences, I promised my dad on what I thought was his deathbed, that if he pulled through, I would do anything. Anything at all—including cutting my hair. My brothers, who were there too, agreed to do the same. It worked! Over the next six months, dad made a complete recovery. My deal long forgotten, I was stunned when my dad announced one Saturday that he remembered the hair deal, and it was the reason he had fought and pulled through. Knowing he could have boys that once again looked like boys instead of girls, he lived. SHIIIITTT!!! I knew what was going to happen next, and it did—flat tops for one and all! I knew even then that a deal was a deal, but I had a sneaking suspicion that he had pulled through for other reasons too. I mean mom was the hottest mom in the neighborhood. I knew this because all of my friends, even in seventh grade, told me so and flirted with her every chance they got as she just laughed them off. I was sure that her movie star looks had something to do with dad recovering. But no, according to dad it was the hair cut deal that did it, and now we had to make good on our promise.

In business, I have learned that not every deal is a good deal. In my early days, I wanted every deal I could get my hands on, regardless of the circumstances. I just wanted to work. It didn't take long before I started getting exactly what I was asking for. Many of the more seasoned speakers tried to warn me. Be careful when you work with this organization or that one—they are not what they seem. I would take speaking jobs that, by the time you figured in my time, the travel etc., ended up with me paying to deliver my own speeches. But I was getting exactly what I asked for.

Today I have learned to do my due diligence. Knowing you usually get what you ask for, I make sure I know exactly what I am asking for before pursuing it. By the way, don't get me wrong. I am glad my dad survived, but I sure hated that haircut. Only good thing about it was that I got that hair cut in June, giving me the summer vacation to at least start working toward cool again.

Points to Ponder

Actor Colin Cunningham said it best: "Be careful what you wish for because you will get it. Be even more careful what you work for because you will get it even more quickly." He is spot on. On my weekly podcast, I wanted to interview one of the older IndyCar drivers, mostly because I wanted to meet him. I got what I asked for. After talking about all his success, I asked him about a big crash he had at Indy one year where is car cartwheeled down the back stretch. A crash he walked away from totally uninjured. I asked, "What was going through your mind and what was happening as you and your car were launched into the air and you began flipping down the backstretch?" He said, "OOOOOOHHHH, I pooped my pants." He got all embarrassed, and his face turned bright red. I said, "Don't be embarrassed, if I myself or any driver was in that same situation, not sure if this was the end or not, I am sure we would poop our pants too." He replied, "No, No, No! Not then. Just a second ago, when I went, OOOOOOHHHH, I pooped my pants." Again, be careful what you ask for cause you just might get it!

CHAPTER 23
BE TIMELESS BUT FRESH

The Indy 500 is always new. Literally every year, the previous owners of the track, the Hulman Family, always gave you something new to get excited about. Every year, they created a new logo for the race, which helped generate millions of dollars in sales for hats, tee shirts, polo shirts, jackets, and all types of trinkets and collectables. Every year, I myself would buy an event tee shirt, a polo shirt, a hat, a program, and flag as soon as they were released months before the race. Recently, while purging old stuff out of the garage, as the wife likes to say, I discovered that over the last 40 years of going to the Indy 500 and IndyCar races in general, I had collected hundreds of event tee shirts, hats, polo shirts, and trinkets. In talking to several of my race buddies, I discovered that I am not the only one who had done so.

In addition, the Hulman's were always upgrading the seating and video screens. A few years ago, when I got to my turn one seats, I was stunned and excited to see the world class upgrades they had made to my section of the track. My new stadium style seats increased the viewing and the comfort by a mile.

The on-track product itself is always new too. Whether it be the speeds, records, or new cars, each year it seems there is something new. Sometimes it's a new world-famous driver, other times it may be a milestone, like the first woman to drive the race, the first African American to drive, or the 100th running. Sometimes it's several of these things all at once. Whatever it is, the Indy 500 is always a new event, and it keeps people coming back. People like being a part of something new, and they like being a part of something special. The Indy 500 is new, special, and so much more every year. It's always a big part of the excitement of going— seeing what's new.

LESSON LEARNED

You have to keep your product fresh and exciting. It may only be minor occasional adjustments, or it may be totally reinventing your product or service from time to time. Indy has taught me that you should view your product or service like a loaf of bread. If it gets stale, people will throw it out for something fresher and more exciting.

PERSONAL STORY

This is one of the most valuable lessons the track has taught me. You see it in business all around you every day. Those who create new products and then constantly strive to update and recreate their products are the ones that truly last. It is no accident that every September Apple introduces updates and totally new designs for its many products. Sometimes these are big changes, other times not so much, but there is always something new. "New" keeps people coming back. I have made that a staple in my business as well. I always am changing and updating the content in my training so that it remains fresh and relevant. I am always the first to market with the way my training is delivered too. As matter of fact, in the last ten years alone, I have updated my training no fewer than nine times, which is a lot, but times are changing at a rapid-fire pace. My customers like new, and I deliver it.

It's not just in business where I practice this either. I have found that "new" keeps relationships fresh and helps them grow stronger. My grandkids are always excited to see me because they never know what "Pop" is going to have for them to do next. Scooters, bikes, walks, swimming, working in the garden? It's always fun, and I know they love it because they always ask when I see them, "What are we going to do today?" with much excitement and anticipation in their young voices. I do the same with friends and especially with my wife. Even though I am sure I do not always accomplish it, I try to make every weekend, every holiday, every vacation different for her. Hiking in Jackson Hole this year, Italy the next, and maybe a big city like New York City after that. As matter of fact, one could say that me being unpredictable is they only thing you can predict about me. I strive to be that way because, just like at the Indianapolis Motor Speedway, new is always fun. New is what people like. The only time my unpredictability was not a hit with my wife was the time I brought home two new, extremely hyperactive Italian Greyhound puppies two weeks before we were to be married. With 15 people scheduled to be sleeping at our house on our wedding weekend and with another 100 scheduled to show up for the wedding, to say she was not excited would be to say it nicely. But hey, I got a good, once in a lifetime deal I just couldn't pass up.

Points to Ponder

Be timeless but fresh. That should be your goal. That is exactly what the Indianapolis Motor Speedway is and that is exactly what the Indy 500 has always been. If you look around you, the biggest companies are just that. Take Apple for instance. With their phones, they took a timeless need—communication—and made it fresh. Uber has done the same thing. Taken a timeless product—travel—and made it fresh. Netflix, likewise, took a timeless product—entertainment—and has made it fresh. In business you learn that the more fresh and new you keep your product, the more your sales will increase. In regard to relationships, my wife recently reignited and freshened up our love life with a new idea. She simply recommended we turn off the lights. She said that I look fresher and newer in the dark.

CHAPTER 24
MEL, JIM AND TOM

MEL KENYON AND JIM HURTIBESE were Indy 500 fan favorites who never won the Indy 500. Although both were outstanding drivers in all types of race cars, winning many races and titles along the way, they just never were able to break through and win the most famous of all races, the Indy 500. They became fan favorites for several reasons. They drove any car anytime they had a chance to on all types of tracks. It was possible to see either or both at a local Midget Car race on Wednesday, in a Sprint Car race on Friday, a Silver Crown car on Saturday, and then either in a NASCAR or IndyCar on Sunday. They raced all across the United States for over two decades and were considered the working man's drivers. But what endeared the fans to them the most was how they would let nothing get in their way of doing what they needed to do. After suffering a fiery crash in 1964, Jim Hurtibese's hands were so badly burnt that the surgeon asked how he would like his hands permanently formed. Jim replied, "Just make 'em so I can hold a steering wheel." The surgeon did, and Jim went on to drive in many more races for another 20 plus years, including either driving in or trying to qualify for 17 more Indy 500s. Mel Kenyon suffered a similar fate. In 1965, Mel was in a racing accident that resulted in the amputation of nearly all his fingers on his left hand. Not to be denied driving race cars, he had a special glove developed that would snap to the steering wheels of his race cars, which allowed him to drive and win so many Midget Car races that he has been named the king of Midget Car racing and as the greatest to ever drive those type of cars. Mel drove in eight more Indy 500s with four top-five finishes and his highest finish of third place in 1968. These guys were loved in and around Indianapolis and everywhere else they drove. These were hard working men that did what they were good at and let nothing stand in their way of competing and supplying for their families. Although, as I have noted previously, my dad was a huge A.J. Foyt fan, and he said more then once, "If A.J can't win today, then I sure hope Kenyon or Hurtibese wins." In those drivers, I think my dad and many like him saw themselves in a big way. They did what had to be done when it needed to be done.

LESSON LEARNED

Doing whatever it takes under any circumstances is one thing that will get you noticed and win you fans. These drivers were thrown huge obstacles that would have been too much to overcome for most. Instead of walking away and being forgotten as someone who had a bad break, Mel and Jim won millions of fans that truly loved them and cheered loudly for them to win every time they got behind the wheel. As a matter of fact, they got many breaks that others never did because they both had proven that they would do whatever it took, no matter the circumstances, to win. They had created the reputation that they would and could get it done. Good things come to those who do not complain as they work toward their goals.

PERSONAL STORY

I got to see firsthand how someone faced struggle, hardship, and especially health issues. My youngest sibling, Tom, was born with Marfan Syndrome. He was nearly five-years-old before we discovered this. Always a clumsy kid, he was always in trouble for running into to stuff, tripping, and mostly for not paying attention. All was a result of his disease that we did not know he had. We made the discovery after he started kindergarten and they found he could not see. As a matter of fact, he was legally blind. At the age of five, he was given glasses so thick that coke bottles were jealous. The optometrist suggested further medical testing, and that is when we uncovered that he had Marfan Syndrome. Marfan syndrome affects the heart, eyes, blood vessels, and bones. Throughout his life, Tom has had the lenses in his eyes removed, has had torn retinas, has had serious heart problems, has had to have his rib cage taken apart and reconstructed in order to make his ribs shorter, has diabetes and cardiovascular disease. Over the past 20 years, he has had both his legs removed. When he was five, we were told he would be lucky to see the age of 12. At the age of 12, they said he would never see 18. At 18, it was pushed to 25. At 25, they said 40. At 40 they said 60, and at 50 they said maybe 70. Thank God for modern medicine.

Where most would have held back, Tom never did. He has lived his life with the attitude, "If it may end soon, what the hell do I have to lose?" He has lived his life with much zest, and he has been someone to look up to. Right up to the time he lost his first leg, he drove a big rig tractor and trailer throughout the continental 48 states hauling produce. On the road for weeks and months at a time, he has seen a lot of stuff. As a matter of fact, he should be writing this book. Infinitely funnier than me and having had a far more interesting life with way better stories, he should be the one writing books. From early on, he feared nothing and was and is a friend to everyone. He has had more girlfriends than any guy has a right to. Even in the condition that he is now, there are women that come visit him all the time and friends from all walks that would do for him whatever he wanted, but he does not ask. He does whatever is needed for himself. Just so the many that know him do not think I am full of it, Tom was no angel. There has been many things he has done to piss plenty of people off with his actions, but at the end of the day, he has lived his life to the fullest, without fear, making many people laugh along the way.

I have always admired and respected Tom. Whenever I woke up and did not feel well, business was bad, the wife was mad, I lost a deal, missed a flight, had a flight cancelled, drove hours to meetings that were cancelled by the time I got there, had no money, or any other insignificant concern, when compared to Tom's daily struggle and being forced to live a life with "just a few more years" in the back of his mind, I figured that if he could do what he was doing, then nothing I was involved in could be even remotely close to what he has had to endure throughout his health challenged life. He has lived harder, has better stories, is funnier, has more luck with the fairer sex, has more friends, can drink anyone under any table anytime, and is mom's favorite. Like Jim and Mel, he won the friendship and love of many by never letting anything like a health issue slow him down and by always doing what others many times would not. That said, I do beat Tom in at least one area. I have a bigger TV with better surround sound.

Points to Ponder

If you wake up and you think you don't feel well, don't have enough energy, don't have what it takes, or you think you just can't get it done today, then simply change your mind.

"Strong minds suffer without complaining; weak minds complain without suffering."

—LETTIE COWMAN

"Champions aren't made in the gyms. Champions are made from something they have deep inside them—a desire, a dream, a vision. They have to have the skill, and the will. But the will must be stronger than the skill."

—MUHAMMAD ALI

"Just make 'em so I can hold a steering wheel,"

—JIM HURTIBESE

CHAPTER 25
BE THE SILVER BULLET

YOU COULD SEE IT HAPPENING right before your eyes. You could see that the very smart, proven past race winner in what many considered at the time, a lesser car on a smaller team, was going to overtake the younger, less experienced driver in the superior car from one of the big teams. A team that had won Indy and other championships numerous times. The younger driver had everything one truly needs in a team- a car and resources, but he lacked experience.

His teammate was Scott Dixon. Scott had won the pole position for the race. Scott was also a six-time series champion and the 2008 Indy 500 race winner. The young driver and Scott were both running for the Chip Ganassi race team. This team that had won 14 championships and five Indy 500s with various drivers over the years. In short, it is a team that is expected to win every time they are on the track.

But this year, the young Alex Paulo in his second Indy 500, who would go onto win the Indy Car Championship later that year, was beaten by the three-time Indy 500 winner Helio

Castroneves. Helio was driving for a growing team for the first time at Indy. All three of Helios previous Indy 500 wins had come while he was driving for the prestigious Penske racing.

In 2020, driver Takuma Sato pulled off a similar feat. Driving for the smaller Rahal Letterman racing team, Sato, who started on the outside of row one, beat Scott Dixon by chasing him down and passing him on lap 172. This was after Scott had led 111 laps of the race after starting in the middle of row one. Even more remarkable was the fact that at one point, Scott led the race by over seven seconds or about 700 yards. That is a big lead at Indy these days. Even though the race ended under the yellow flag after a huge crash elsewhere in the field, it was clear that no one was going to catch Sato. This was the second Indy 500 win for Sato. He had also won the race in 2017, while driving for the Andretti racing team.

In 2013 Tony Kanaan, an Indy Car champion and multiple race winner, gave the really small team of KV racing their very first Indy Car race win of any type by winning that year's Indy 500 in dramatic fashion. It is worth noting that, as I pointed out in chapter 19, the 2013 Indy 500 is considered by most to be the toughest Indy 500 ever run with more passes and less yellow flags than any other Indy 500.

I could note and share similar stories about team owners, the engineers, and countless others who have been a major factor to success, in, around, and on the track. Consider Bryan Herta. He was an integral part of the 2011 and 2016 victories. He played an invaluable role in getting the drivers across the finish line to experiencing the sweet taste of victory milk.

In 2011, Bryan Herta Autosport, had a technical alliance with the Indy Car team, Vision Racing. With driver Dan Wheldon, Herta won the Indy 500 on his first try and as his first race as a team owner. In 2016 he repeated the feat by partnering his one car team with Andretti Auto Sports. Herta won the race as an owner for a second time with Indy 500 rookie, Andre Rossi. It should be noted that Andretti Racing ran four other cars of their own with more experienced teams and some of the top drivers in the sport at the time, but it was Herta and Rossi that celebrated in the winner's circle.

It can't be overstated that the one consistency in all of Team Penske's 18 Indy 500 victories is Roger Penske, himself. Like all the forementioned people, Roger is the silver bullet- the magical solution to a complicated problem- that makes his team a threat for the win every single time they take to the track.

With all of these people, you can see in their walk and their talk, they mean business. You feel the intensity when you are near them at the track. They all come across as fun loving and nice people, but you clearly get the sense that when they are at the track, they are focused on one thing and one thing only – winning. They show up to work and focus on the job at hand. Of course, they want to win for themselves, but you can see by the way they interact with others that they understand their role has a much grander scope. They see that the big picture is about much more than themselves. It is about the entire team, the sponsors, the fans, their families, and the many committed others who count on them to perform at the highest levels.

When you listen to them in interviews, they take full responsibility for missteps and direct accolades to everyone but themselves when things go right. In these interviews, they talk only about getting to the front, staying there, and winning. They never doubt themselves and they never doubt their teams or their supporters. They may say that an event is going to be tough, but they always reinforce that they are there to win and will do everything in their earthy power to make that win a reality. You believe them.

It makes no difference whether they are starting first or last. If they are the fastest or slowest. If they have been struggling or cruising. They always talk within the framework of winning. They love what they are doing and they are totally committed to being the best they can be for themselves and even more so, for the many who count on them.

Although I have never heard any of these men refer to themselves as the silver bullet, they clearly are what made the difference when it counted. All types have come to Indy with varying degrees of success. A good finish here, a fast car there, and sometimes even win or two. What they lacked was the consistency needed to become a champion, not just a one-time-wonder, but a champion and winner, over and over again. That kind of success requires looking outward and beyond self-interests. That kind of success is derived by developing a keen understanding of all the parts and how they work together. It is making yourself the silver bullet.

Lesson Learned

To achieve the level necessary to participate in Indy Car, you personally have to strive and sacrifice to get there. Many who get there are so focused on the struggle in getting there, that they forget to shift gears and start doing what it takes to propel them to the next level- the big picture level required for consistent Indy success. Lost and without a plan, they begin to see others successes as lucky breaks, or some kind of secret silver bullet.

They forget that they got to where they are by persistence and hard work. Not luck or chance. They must examine the challenges of reaching higher levels of success and use the same dedication and tenacity they have used all along, to propel them to their next objective. It is not necessary to reinvent the wheel to reach loftier goals, you simply have to do the things that others before you did and improve upon them. Incorporate your own work ethic and experience, with an understanding of what it takes to be the best. This comes from studying those who have been successful in your field. Use their methods and put your stamp on it. Make it better. You can't give up believing in yourself. You have to embrace the challenge at this stage and become the silver bullet. To keep the momentum going and to keep moving up and into the winners circle, keep believing and acting like you are the silver bullet. The hard work, dedication, and knowledge that got you to this place, will continue to propel you to the checkered flag and into the winners circle forever.

The Indy 500 has taught me that you can show up and spend your time at the track looking for the silver bullet, or you can become the silver bullet and be the one that others are searching for.

PERSONAL STORY

Although I used more recent personalities and events in the proceeding story, my silver bullet theory is one that I picked-up on from my earliest days of watching and attending the Indy 500. For example, AJ Foyt has won four Indy 500s. He is the only driver to win the race in both a front and rear engine car. He won it when he was a driver on a team owned by another and as a driver on his own team. He then won Indy as a team owner with a driver he hired. Coincidence? I think not.

Bobby Unser, Al Unser Sr., and Al Unser Jr., total nine Indy 500s between them. What is remarkable is that those nine wins came from eight different teams. Coincidence?

And it goes on and on. Just like in most sports, there are dominant teams and players, but there are many more who are barely remembered. It became very apparent to me that winning consistently almost always came from an individual who was in, on, or around those teams. Although it takes a team to win, it also takes an individual that is unique – a silver bullet.

I studied and still study these individuals and have uncovered the key elements to their formula to becoming the difference makers:

1. Passion-When these winners are in the game, preparing for and playing that game consumes their lives. It is the one thing they live for. They will go anywhere, anytime, and do anything within the limits of the law to play the game. It is their passion and who they are.

2. Dedication- Silver bullet types don't allow anyone or anything to stand in their way. Complete dedication to the goal is required. It is clear when you are around them that you must be part of the solution, if you want to stay. The minute you become part of the problem or a distraction, you will be cut from their circle of influence.

3. Risk taker- They are willing to play not just the long shot, but the long, long shot. They do not see risk, as risk as much as they see it as a challenge and a bridge leading to a higher level.

4. Open-minded - They will take a chance with something less for less if they believe it will ultimately get them something more. Helio's fourth win at Indy, Wheldon's second win and Kanaan's lone Indy win came from each of them driving on a smaller budget team while being paid a fraction of what they were used to. Each knew the first step to winning any race is first making the field.

5. Embrace responsibility- Successful people in the racing industry clearly understand that in order to make a car go fast, they first have to be able to communicate to the team why the car is currently not going fast. They also understand that sometimes the missing piece will come from an engineer who uncovers something in the data that

will generate speed. It may be a driving teammate who uncovers the way to get that extra 100th of a second. Smart leaders listen. They take advice. They even seek advice. But at the end of the day, they know that car is fast or it is not because of them. It won or it did not win because of them. They accept the results. They listen, they learn, and they make the changes necessary to do better, go faster, and win. They thrive on the responsibility. It is part of what creates the adrenaline that winners crave.

I have always approached my business like I am the silver bullet. I have been the one constant throughout its 36 year life. I was there for every failure and I have been there for every win. I love what I do and it shows. As a matter of fact, I am mostly described as a passionate speaker more than anything else.

I am dedicated and will go anywhere, anytime, to deliver a speech or a presentation. I have been on stage on my birthday, anniversary, and holidays. I give presentations on Saturdays, Sundays, early in the day and late at night. I have had great positions and the worst positions on agendas. Makes no difference to me. I love what I do and I do it for myself, and the many behind the scenes that depend on me.

In my business risk is a big part of the game. I have flown half way around the world on my own dime to speak for just 30 minutes on stages that I felt warranted the risk. Sometimes it works out and I sign big contracts while other times, I return home unsuccessful. I learn from it and move on. I have had more products fail than succeed. I am comfortable with that since you have to know what does not work to learn what does.

I have always been open-minded. I remember one time when I was invited to be part of a five-speaker roster. All the speakers were equal in stature and popularity. It was an excellent opportunity. An opportunity that would allow the presenters to showcase their abilities. The question was, who would go on first and who would headline? After an hour of listening to the others argue their case for headliner, I willingly took the opening spot and proceeded to fine tune my presentation to the point where no one wanted to follow me. I did that event five consecutive years and each time was voted the best speaker of the day. Since that time, I have had entered into many agreements as a speaker only if I could be the opener. I can headline, but I have no problem being an opener. Being flexible and versatile has proved to be very rewarding.

Another cavate I have written into my agreements is that, if times permits, I like to arrive a day early to rehearse. Although I have been on thousands of stages many times presenting the same material, I never leave anything to chance. I want to see the room and the stage. I want to know how many stairs there are to getting on stage. I want to know about the lighting, technology, and the sound system. How will the seats be arranged? I take nothing for granted and I take everything seriously. There are two main reasons I do that. First, I feel that if a group of people are going to give me their time and attention, I owe it to them to be the absolute best I can be. And second, there is a whole team of people behind me that have real families and real mortgages and real lives. They are counting on me to give my all so that they can continue to provide for their own lives. It is my number one responsibility to be the best possible for them and I embrace that responsibility, whole-heartedly.

I have learned over time that I can be the lead bullet or I can be the silver bullet in what makes me successful in what I do. If you incorporate the elements of the formula laid out here, becoming the silver bullet is not only easier, it is more interesting and rewarding. You can waste your time chasing the elusive silver bullet that it seems only the winners have or you can spend your time becoming the silver bullet that everyone else chases to the winners circle.

POINTS TO PONDER

One of the things that I have never understood is why so many people accept what is happening around them simply because it is happening. Just because sales are slow in your industry or at your company does not mean your personal sales have to be slow, too. When you accept the norm as the norm you are now acting like a lead bullet. A big heavy lead bullet that lacks speed and accuracy. You have become part of the problem and not part of the solution. Those who approach a problem or a challenge as just that, are the ones who become the true winners.

Winners know that every problem, challenge, or concern has a solution or more than one solution. They don't waste their time fretting, worrying, or allowing things to hold them back or bring them down. On some level, they get excited by the obstacles knowing that once they uncover the solution(s), the result will be moving ahead of your competitors. Once out front they make it to the winners circle like a speeding bullet, a silver bullet.

While it may be popular to believe that there are no silver bullets in life, I disagree. I believe silver bullets are everywhere and have names. In Indy Car the names on the silver bullets are Andretti, Sato, Penske, Ganassai, Castroneves, Foyt, Unser, and Herta to name a few. The list certainly does not stop there. In your world there are silver bullets and you can become one, too. It is as simple as stopping the search for one and becoming one. You and you alone, most likely, are the silver bullet you have been looking for.

CHAPTER 26
ROGER PENSKE

ROGER PENSKE IS AN INSPIRATION. I must admit, I have cheered for him and against him. I have rooted for his drivers and against them. I have been in the camp that believes his resources may have given him an unfair advantage, and I have also been stunned by how much he has helped others with those very same resources. I'm describing my feelings here. Good, bad, for, against. These are all feelings and feelings are rooted in emotion. Many times, emotions can cloud the truth. So, trusting the feelings becomes complicated.

When you strip away the emotion and look at and analyze the facts regarding Mr. Penske, you will find him to be in the simplest language, a man that does what he says he will do, and does what he is supposed to do.

He came to Indianapolis and dominated the month many times, with a dream team of drivers. This caused other teams to wonder how he did it? Fact is, that's what he was supposed to do. There were years when he came to Indy and things did not work out well. He handled those situations with class and distinction because fact is, that is what real winners are supposed to do.

Mr. Penske has hired winning drivers away from smaller teams and fired big time drivers because they could win no more. He knows what he is supposed to do and he does it. When he added and subtracted cars to and from his team, it may have been seen as the thing not to do, but he knew what was necessary and he did it. He did what he was supposed to do.

Although I have never witnessed it, there are rumors that say you don't want to be in the Penske garage at the end of a bad day at the track, especially if the bad day was caused by a team member or driver who dropped the ball. Sometimes Mr. Penske is supposed to be that guy, too. The guy who lets you know you messed up.

Throughout my career, I have had the opportunity to work with some of Penske's automotive dealerships. They too, are run just like his race team. Everything is spick and span. Employees are dressed impeccably, and all who work in these dealerships are held accountable to perform at the highest levels, if they desire to remain on the Penske team. When the employees talk about working with Mr. Penske, they tell you that he is tough and demanding, but he is fair. I have yet to meet an employee who feared him, but they all seem to highly respect him and enjoy working with him. That is the way it is supposed to be.

Although it is simply stated, doing what you are supposed to do is actually hard to come by. We live in a world where everyone seems to want what they want, and they want it right now. Little effort and sacrifice is made on their part. Not Mr. Penske. He has built his business with a slow courageous hand. He had a clear vision and surrounding himself with a team of people who were committed and delivered on that vision. They committed to him because he followed through on his commitment to them. This reciprocal relationship built a solid worldwide brand that is one of the most respected in the industry. If a product or service says Penske on it, you know it will do what it is supposed to do and so much more.

That is why I and so many of the fans are excited that Mr. Penske is now the owner of the Indianapolis Motor Speedway, the Indy 500, and the Indy Car racing series. Who knows? It may be his destiny to take stewardship of these national treasures or fate. Whatever the reason, it has happened and we are excited . We are excited because of what he has promised to do with these national institutions. He has vowed to make them bigger and better and, in fact, he already has. But according to him, he is not yet done.

It is thrilling to see what he is doing and what he will do. It is awe inspiring to witness, especially when you factor in that he is doing it at the age of 85 with a level of enthusiasm and energy that most people lose by the time they are 40.

LESSON LEARNED

Success certainly takes a little luck, but Mr. Penske has proven that you can create luck for yourself. His secret seems to be that he uncovers what others want and/or need. He promises to deliver it better than anyone else can and then delivers it. Usually, better than anyone could have imagined. Mr. Penske has created such a powerful brand and reputation over his long storied career, that when his name is tied to any project, people want to be involved. Some might look at his professional career and attribute his success to how long he has been in business. The thought being that by hanging in there, he was bound to be successful. But the facts show something very different. By following his formula, he was successful at a very young age, continued to be successful through middle age, and now is proving it can even be done in the twilight years. His success is by design, not luck. Figure out what people want or need. Promise to do it better than anyone else. And then, do it better than anybody ever imagined it could be done. That is what you are supposed to do and should do if you want to join Mr. Penske in the winner's circle of life and business.

Personal Story

When I got my first professional sales job, I knew I was out of my league. The sales team consisted of over 80 people and they all appeared to be highly skilled and well prepared. I also noticed, that only about 20% of them were making any real money, and less than 10% of them were making the BIG bucks.

Although I had been given the same training as the rest of the team, I was not exactly sure how to use it. I wanted the BIG money and I believed what they had told me in training. It did not take years or seniority to make be successful. What it took was hard work, dedication, a strong desire to succeed, and the willingness to do what was needed to be done, when it needed to be done. I could do that. It was at a time in my life when I was single. I had nothing better to do than to drink until last call every night. Since my liver and wallet had recently told me they needed a serious break, it was the perfect time for me to become what it took to be a top performer and earner.

This is where I literally took a page right of what I imagined was Mr. Penske's book of knowledge and success. First, I decided that it would be fruitless to take any advice or copy anything that the bottom 90% were doing. They were more than willing to give me advice. I was cordial when they gave it and then I promptly ignored it, since most of their advice was laced with excuses and how hard it was to be successful.

I then turned my attention to the top ten percent. They had the secrets and answers I needed, but much to my dismay, they were not excited about sharing. They would help me if asked, but only sparingly. This limited information helped me, but it was not enough for me to equal or outperform them. I quickly caught on to their game and I did the next best thing I could do, I studied them. I noted when they came into work and when the left. I studied what they did. I listened to them talk to the managers, the owners, and especially to past customers and prospects. I paid attention to how they dressed, what kind of cars they drove. I listened to how they interacted with the office staff, warehouse staff, and everyone else who worked in the place. When I was lucky enough to be invited out to a social event where I knew they would be in attendance, I watched how they interacted with the others in the room and watched how they treated each other, their friends outside of work, and how they treated their significant others. I listened to them talk about their business, personal, and life goals and how they planned to achieve them. It didn't take long for me to gather my initial intel, and once I had it, I emulated their behaviors and business practices. Within a few months, I was firmly in the top 10%. I did not have to reinvent the wheel, I just figured out what made the wheel spin the fastest and I copied it. Throughout the company, people were surprised at how I went from being in the bottom 80% in my first month, to the top 50% in month two, and to the top 10% in my third month. But I was not done. I not only wanted to be in the top 10%, I wanted to be in the top 1%, as in number one!

My next step was to find out what the others in the top ten were doing wrong or what they were doing that could be improved upon. After all, they were not gods, they were salespeople, just like me. I sensed that they were beatable and I was right. Actually, it didn't require making big changes to beat them. It came to me in small efforts and the little details. I came in 30 minutes earlier than anyone else and was always the last to leave, save management and ownership. Sometimes, if the opportunity presented itself, I even stayed and engaged with management. I tweaked our follow-up system for non-buyers and buyers alike. At the time, we could earn up to 50% of the commission from any deal if another salesperson was having trouble and invited you into the sale or handed it off to you to help close. I made it my rule to be involved in more handoffs than anyone else. Others wanted nothing to do with handoffs because they wanted all or nothing. I quickly became the guy that people went to most for handoff sales. Fifty percent is better than zero percent, anytime. I positioned myself to having 30% of my monthly income earned from handoffs. The next closest to this number in the top 10% earned 5% of their income this way.

There are other things that I did that others were not doing or were not willing to do. The point is that what I was doing was what Roger Penske was doing. I did what was promised and expected and I did it better than anyone else. It only took six months to reach the top and by the end of my first 12 months with the company I was number one. The crazy thing about all of this was that by the time I got everything figured out and set up, I was only working an average of two to three more hours a week than the rest of the sales team.. That put in me in a position to earn 30% more than the number two salesperson.

Once everyone else figured out what I was doing to make all this happen, they started to copy me. It did make things tougher, but by the time they figured it out, I was so far ahead of the game, they could not catch me. A few got close, a few beat me here and there, but no one ever knocked me off the throne. Here is what is even crazier, I truly believe that there were at least 15 other people on that staff that had more skill than I did. They simply were not willing to consistently do what it took to be at the top of the board.

Looking back, I can identify three things that helped me to accomplish, maintain, and improve upon my goals. Once I accomplished my goals, I was able to maintain and improve them.

1. I believed ownership and my managers when they told me I had to work hard, be dedicated, have a strong desire to

succeed, and possess the willingness to do what needed to be done, when it needed to be done. I did that.

2. I watched and learned from the winners. When I started winning I continued to watch them and I continued to look in the mirror on a daily, weekly, monthly, and annual basis. I was always asking myself, "What could I do better?" "Where could I improve?" "Are there any opportunities I was missing?" I also shared all of my knowledge, systems, and processes fully with anyone who asked for them.

3. I constantly tried to uncover what the business owners, managers and most importantly, the customers wanted. Once I uncovered that, I sold them on the fact that I would deliver it better than anyone else, and I did that, to the best of my ability.

I am no Roger Penske, but I took a page from his playbook and did what I was supposed to do and became very successful doing it.

Points to Ponder

I have been very fortunate in my personal and business life to have witnessed many award ceremonies and sporting events. I am never surprised at how the winners of business awards, sporting events and even championships, respond to the simple question, "How do you do get to the winners circle so often?" If you listen, somewhere in the answer you will almost always hear, "It's what I am supposed to do and I am paid to do. I do it for the owners. I do it for my managers. I do it for our team. And, I mostly do it for the fans/customers."

If you study the "greatest generation" from WWII and asked them why they made such great sacrifices, the most common answer you will get is, "It was what I was supposed to do." And they did it, better than anyone else ever imagined.

When you agree to work for another, if true security and reward is what you seek, the answer will be found in uncovering what the business owner needs and delivering that better than anyone else could ever imagine. If you travel down the road of owning your own business, your job will be to surround yourself with great people and deliver to them what you promised on a level that exceeds their expectations.

The true and consistent winners in life are only slightly different than the unsuccessful. The consistently successful work hard, are dedicated, have a strong desire to succeed and the willingness to do what is needed to be done when it is needed to be done. They do what they are supposed to do and usually more than they are paid to do.

Whatever your goal in life, you must define it, define the steps to make it happen, and then go about making it happen. You simply have to do what you are supposed to do better than anyone else ever imagined. Exceed expectations. This will create a lifetime of security and happiness. You need to look no further than to the great man who has the owners suite at 16th and Georgetown Road in Indianapolis, Indiana. Roger Penske did what he was supposed to do, exceeding the expectations of others. He did it. You can do it. And you can take comfort in knowing that it's what you are supposed to do.

CHAPTER 27
KNOW THE RIGHT TIME TO LET GO

WHEN TONY HULMAN PURCHASED the Indianapolis Motor Speedway from Eddie Rickenbacker in 1945, it was with the intense excitement of knowing that he could take something that was once great and make it even greater. And make it greater is precisely what he did. I am sure, as a businessman, he saw the potential for massive profit, but throughout his life, one got the sense that the longer he owned it, the less it became about profit and the more it became about the important race held their annually.

As the years passed, his enthusiasm for future races grew exponentially. He strove to make every edition better than the last. Better racing surfaces, better grandstands, better fan experiences, and better exposure. Everything was improved upon, made bigger and better than the previous year. Although he owned several businesses, it appeared to all that the one thing that Mr. Human really lived for was the Indianapolis Motor Speedway and the Greatest Spectacle in Racing – The Indy 500. Through his ownership, it became legendary and the Indy 500 still maintains the status of being the biggest single day sporting event on the worldwide sports calendar each year. After his passing in 1977, his wife, Mary, carried on with the same high level of commitment and love for the race as her husband had before her. After her mother's passing in 1998, Mari Hulman-George (Mary and Tony's daughter) continued the family's tradition of excellence that was set by her parents. Mari turned over the reins of the historic place to her son, Tony George. Initially, Tony seemed to have the necessary devotion and understanding of the business, the track, and the event, to follow in the footsteps of his grandparents and mother. That changed however, when Tony began listening to the fans and started an all-oval track series known as the Indy Racing League or simply the IRL. On paper, it looked to be a great idea and exactly what the fans wanted. But when put to practice, it split Indy Car racing in half. All but one of the big well-funded teams, A.J. Foyt Racing, left and went their own way, leaving Tony George to literally start a new series from the ground up. The only thing that he had was the famous track and race that his family owned. Without those two key ingredients, the new league would have folded in its first year. Instead, it lasted for just over a decade.

From 1997 through 2008, Tony's racing series hosted some of the most hair raising, close open wheel events that have rarely been witnessed before or since. Although the racing was tight and seemed to be exactly what fans cried about wanting for years leading up to the formation of the new league, most of the more recognizable drivers stayed away, and mostly because of that, so did the fans.

Other tracks that the Indy Cars raced on that once drew 50,000 to 100,000 fans could barely draw 15,000 to 20,000 fans. The same thing happened with the other side, Champ Car series, where most of the big teams and more recognizable drivers drove. Although, when all the teams came back together in 2008 to what is now known simply as Indy Car Racing, several team owners and drivers took responsibility and the rightful blame for the split. Tony George was the one individual whose name, reputation, and power was most in jeopardy. The fans felt that he was the sole reason for a split that took Indy Car from one of the top racing series that drew huge crowds and television ratings, to an event that was barely on the radar screen, save for the Indianapolis 500.

With his power gone and his image diminished, Tony stepped aside. From that point, it appeared that the Hulman-George family had relinquished the throne to any and everything Indy 500. Tony was the heir apparent and with no others in the family wanting to take over the reins, it was really only a matter of time before one of two things happened. Either the Indy 500 and Indy Car would diminish into a thing of the past, or the family would sell.

Luckily for the millions and millions of fans worldwide, the family knew the importance of what the track, the series, and the main race meant to the sporting and racing world. The family understood the significance of the rich traditions and history of the race and what those traditions meant to the city of Indianapolis, the state of Indiana, and the United States. They seemed to be fully aware of the fact that they were seen as the family who would ran Indy into the ground and out of business. They were the family that knew it was time to exit and find someone to take over, someone who had the same level of enthusiasm for the track like Carl Fisher, Eddie Rickenbacker, and Tony Hulman had when they were the ones in charge.

The family knew it was time to exit. They knew that the track, the series, and the Indy 500 had become bigger than any one family or individual. They knew that for the track and race to survive and thrive, it needed to be owned and cared for by an entity that could rekindle the commitment, vision, and excitement of the original owners. They set their egos aside and placed their family legacy into the hands of another. I am sure they made a handsome profit when the sold the track, but walking away from 16th Street and Georgetown road in Indianapolis, had to be very painful. The racing world and all of the fans are grateful to the Hulman family for recognizing a difficult challenge and making the right choice. That took guts.

LESSON LEARNED

Knowing what is needed to make a sale, lead a team, or run a business is critical if you want to remain relevant, profitable, and at the top. Although an individual or team of individuals may be an important component in the success of a business and its products, their involvement, commitment, and enthusiasm must remain at a high level for that business and product to continue to grow and flourish. If any of those things start to diminish on any level, that is the first sign that it may be time to do a self-examination and either recommit, or to step aside and allow others to take over the reins. Fail to do so and you risk becoming obsolete, a business that holds no interest and is no longer wanted or needed.

Personal Story

Throughout my 36-year career as a business owner, one of the hardest things I have learned to do is to let go of different aspects of the business, even when it is clear to me that the letting go is the best thing to do.

My company started out with me being primarily a one person show. As my business and its products and services became more popular, I had to bring in more people to help me. Each time I did, I had to let something go that I had done previously on my own. Sometimes that was easy. Most of the time it was hard.

Letting go of the paperwork, for example, was easy simply because I hate the minutia of paperwork. On the other hand, letting go of digging for new prospects, making sales presentations to earn new clients, and closing new deals was hard to delegate. Although I still do some of that, it is more of an advisory role for me now. My sales team prefers I let them do what I pay them to do and stay out of the new deals – their words.

It's the same when it comes to visiting businesses and coaching the employees. That too, grew to a point where I needed more and more people to help. After over 15 years of non-stop travel and personally visiting over 700 businesses, it was pointed out to me that it would be better for the company if I gave that up and became a public speaker. I did not like this idea. It was like someone was ripping my heart out. But my best clients started asking that I not return, and instead send my hired coaches. The reason was that since I was the owner of what was no longer a small company, and because I had become quite well known in the industry, many people were intimidated by my presence and felt inhibited. Not the atmosphere we were trying to achieve.

This was and still is hard for me to believe, since I have always seen myself as a simple Indiana boy just trying to earn a living. But a funny thing happens when your products are recorded and your video training and books that are sold on Amazon and at books stores. People start to see you on a TV screen and read your books, and they start to see you more as a "personality" than a simple guy.

Even though I wrestled with having to give up the visits to individual businesses, I knew that it was time to move on and do what was best for my company, especially for the many who are dedicated and work for me. As a matter of fact, if it was not for that reason alone, I probably would not have given it up. Many times, like in the selling of the Indianapolis Motor Speedway, IndyCar and essentially the Indy 500, stepping away and moving on is what is best for everyone.

In life I have learned to follow my gut and my instincts. They might not always lead you to where you want to go, but if you listen and pay attention, they will almost always lead you to where you need to go.

POINTS TO PONDER

Stepping away, moving on, distancing yourself, or whatever you want to call it, is hard to do. This is particularly true if you have built a thing, been tied to it, or associated with it for many years. It is a part of you and letting go of something that is a part of you changes you forever. The longer you have been connected to something, the harder it is to let go.

The formidable blocker to letting go is emotion. When I moved from working with one business at a time to becoming a public speaker and working with hundreds at a time, it was clear to everyone but me that I was making the smart move. What made it hard was my emotional tie to working one on one with people. It was who I was. It was my identity. It was what I enjoyed most and now I was being asked to step away from that into the public speaking arena, something I was not sure at the time was going to work. I actually fought it.

But, once I analyzed it, weighing the pros and cons, and removed the emotional component, I knew it was the right thing for my business. I have discovered that the more a person feels, the less they think. You have to eliminate emotion when making business decisions. Sentimentality will not get you where you need to go. Clear, informed, and practical thinking will guide you to success in business. Of course, following your instinct has to be included in this process, but instinct rarely requires emotions. Instinct comes from experience and experience is a great teacher.

Every single time in my life, whether it be personal orbusiness, when my gut tells me change is in the air, once I sideline the emotion and take the jump, it almost always works out the way I want it to. To step aside and let go, one has to be brave. My focus is always on the greater good my bravery will bring to others, and to myself. Be brave. When the moment dictates and let go. Have your radar up for when these moments present themselves. Don't turn away from challenges. Lean into them. Even if it is a small step, take it. The smallest steps many times result in the biggest leaps forward and it's only in letting go that we can truly make those giant leaps.

CHAPTER 28
THE UNDERDOG IS THE TOP DOG

WHEN YOU DRIVE FOR ONE OF THE "BIG TEAMS," the expectation is that you will win poles, run up front all day, and ultimately win races. For the most part, that is exactly what takes place. Few are surprised when these expectations are realized. And they are in most seasons in most races.

However, what also happens every season at some races is that the underdog shows up and soundly beats the top teams and drivers. At the 100th running of the Indy 500, Andre Rossi was driving in his first Indy 500 on a one-off team and was considered a long shot underdog right up to the moment when he crossed the finish line first and won the race. The crowd was stunned, almost as much as the other teams and drivers he beat.

It seems every year on bump day, when there are more than 33 cars vying to qualify for the race, some underdog shocks the crowd and steals a spot from a more experienced, better funded team and driver.

The longest running underdog who shows up year after year with sometimes what is less than half the budget of the big teams is owner, driver, Ed Carpenter. Ed has Indy consistently dialed in, especially on Pole Day. To make matters worse for the better funded teams and drivers, Ed used to be a threat in one car. Now he shows up with two additional cars and sometimes two fearless drivers who were passed over by the big teams. He is no longer a one car threat, but a three car threat.

Ed and his team may not be a major concern at every track, but they certainly are at Indy. Every year it seems, especially on Pole Day when it truly matters, Ed puts his Chevy so far out on the edge, it is frightening. In the last ten years, he started the race from the pole position three times, second only to seven-time series champion and 2008 Indy 500 winner, Scott Dixon. Ed's team has started on the front row seven times during that ten years. Although Ed and his drivers have not won the great spectacle, they do stay up front and most of the time can be seen leading the race for many laps at a time.

Year after year, Ed and his team arrive on the scene and are always cast as underdogs. It must be incredibly frustrating for the much larger teams, who have the best engineers, mechanics, pit crews, and drivers, to routinely have Ed and his crew show up and give them a real run for their money. Ed has recently withdrawn himself from driving every race in the series and now runs only the ovals. His other drivers typically run the full season. You get the sense that the competitors and many fans wonder just how long this underdog can keep up this kind of performance at Indy.

I believe Ed Carpenter and his team will perform this way as long as he has the desire to do so. You see, Ed has never seen himself as an underdog. Ed is not intimidated by any of the other drivers or teams. He respects them immensely and races them as clean as a driver can, but he is not intimidated. That is made very clear when you listen to Ed and his team on the racing radios. Fans who have these radios can tune in to hear the drivers talk to their teams. It gives fans an inside seat to the racing drama. To say that Ed is intense is a huge understatement.

Ed shows up with his team every year and expects his team to sit on the pole, lead the race, and win it. Ed doesn't think like an underdog. He doesn't act like an underdog, and he doesn't race like an underdog. That's what makes him so good at Indy. The secret sauce for Ed is to not listen to others and not succumb to the underdog mentality. He knows what he is. He is a hard charging, intelligent, clean driver who shows up well prepared for the task at hand.

I saw Ed beat three-time Indy 500 champion Dario Franchitti by inches at the finish line in Kentucky and I saw Ed beat him again on the high banks of Fontana. Both times, Dario was at the peak of his career and driving for one of the big teams. Both times, in the closing laps of those races, Ed had the crowd on their feet and in near hysterics as he raced across the finish line first to take the checkered flag. The crowd reacts with the same kind of enthusiasms each time he takes the lead at Indy. We yell, scream, and desperately hope that the local boy from Indianapolis, who is always humble and never brags, stays up front long enough to get the win at the greatest spectacle in racing. If that reality ever comes to pass, I am certain there will be cheering so loud that citizens around the world will instantly know and forever remember the moment when the underdog won. When he beat the top dogs and drove straight to the winners circle. He never sees himself as anything other than a grand champion that could be best in show.

Lesson Learned

Underdogs serve a great purpose. They remind many of us who may have fewer resources, less experience, and opportunities that we can win in any situation, if we do the following:

1. Believe in yourself.
2. Do not allow others to define you.
3. Prepare for opportunity so that when it comes, you are ready.
4. Don't be intimidated by those who have more resources, more experience, and more opportunity.
5. Remind yourselves that the greatest weakness of the most successful is that they do not take the underdog seriously. This is why they are always so surprised when they get beat by one. Use your situation to your own advantage.
6. Focus on using your resources, your talent, and your dedication to catapult you to beating your competition. Don't think about what you don't have. Cultivate your strengths.

PERSONAL STORY

One of my favorite moments in owning my own business was when I went head-to-head with several, well established training companies to secure some very large contracts with a few select auto manufacturers. In the early 2,000's, I was invited to prepare a proposal and make a presentation to the Nissan Motors Company's vice president in charge of training and her team. This was a monster opportunity and certainly the most significant one I had up to that point.

When the day arrived, I walked into the Nissan offices and my heart immediately sank. As I was walking in, the sales team for the biggest automotive training company at the time was walking out. They looked like they had just slayed a dragon. One of them even asked their colleague what I was doing there? The reply was that I was there to embarrass myself.

To make matters worse, a few minutes later when I entered the presentation room, I noticed that at least two other big training firms had made presentations earlier. Their handouts had been left on the podium. I felt outclassed and started wondering what I was I doing there. I was the underdog by a wide margin and felt like one.

Miraculously, fate intervened. As I was going through my briefcase, gathering the materials for my presentation, I noticed a headline from the sports page of a newspaper I had stuffed in my case that morning. The headline read, "Underdog Steals the Show at Indy Qualifying!" It hit me like a ton of bricks. Whether I was the underdog or not, my job was now to convince everyone in the room that I was the best. My job was to dismiss the idea of being an underdog and to convince the team that I was the best for the job. I did just that, and here is how I did it.

At the end of my presentation, I flipped the script and made the others the underdog. I told Nissan that I knew that the other three competitors were bigger, had more assets, and more resources. I pointed out that I knew their presentation materials may have looked fancier and flashier. They may have even have sounded more confident. I pointed out that their business suits were probably more expensive than mine. I acknowledged that in the presentation room, they may have looked and sounded better, but that is where it ended. I explained that where it truly mattered, I was going to bring the desired results. I asked them to answer the following: Who can deliver content that ensures the highest level of employee and customer satisfaction? Who has the best processes that have been proven in thousands of businesses? Who has a product that consistently is recognized for delivering the highest profit margins? These are the only questions to consider when making a selection. When they answered these questions, it would show my company as anything but the underdog in the real world where it counts.

Our training was developed by people who have done the jobs they are teaching. This has provided them with real knowledge in real time in real businesses with real employees, and real customers. I showed that if they were looking for training that would consistently deliver the highest return on their investment, I was the only choice.

I have been in enough of these meetings to know that at the start, there are always favorites and there are always underdogs. I am willing to admit that in situations like this, I most likely appear as the underdog. I don't have the fanciest handouts. I don't have the slickest presentation software, and I certainly do not have the priciest suits. What I do have, that no one else has, is a track record that shows consistent, desired results. Big results. Results that are real. Results that matter. Results that will turn the heads of all who experience them. Results that will solve problems and then some. Results that I will gladly and openly put up against any of my competitors, regardless of market share. Results that no one can match. Some may have seen me as an underdog, and that is fair. But out in the real world, where it counts, Jeff Cowan's Pro Talk is anything but an underdog. Our results make us leaders in the field.

Within 24 hours, I was invited to present a test workshop. Within a week of doing so, I was awarded the contract. It was my first million-dollar deal. It was supposed to be for one calendar year, but after the first year, we negotiated for six more calendar years. That agreement only ended when I decided I wanted to come off the road from doing as many workshops as the agreement required. I had recently gotten married and wanted to spend more time at home with my new bride.

Ironically, after a 13 year break, Nissan and I are happily working together again. It seems history is pleasantly repeating itself. After completing an agreement with them in 2022, we have secured a new contract for 2023, and beyond.

POINTS TO PONDER

At some point in your life, you will be the underdog. The unknown entity that arrives on the scene seemingly out of nowhere. The one who must prove themselves. Your first day on a job. Your first day in a vocational school, or college. Your first day as a parent. These are all situations that put you squarely in the underdog arena.

It is not only being new at something that gets you this title. I have known and do know others in the sales profession and in business who are underdogs and have been all their lives. This is due to the size of their resources, products, location, or countless other factors. I myself started out being an underdog and am still considered one most of the time. It doesn't bother me. I doubt that it ever will. My success gives me confidence.

You are only a true underdog if you allow yourself to be one. It took guts to say what I said at the Nissan meeting. It was edgy, and if delivered the wrong way, could have come off as very pompous. But being the underdog has its advantages. When you are the underdog, most of the time you have little to lose and much to gain. I get a big kick out of surprising people with the products, services, and results I provide to my clients. I feel most alive when I am considered the underdog. Nothing to lose, everything to gain. The surprise they feel when I prove them wrong is incredibly motivating. My adrenaline starts pumping just thinking about it.

In the end, underdogs are needed in sales, in business, and in life. Underdogs inspire and remind us that if we think we can, we can! Underdogs remind the big dogs that they can be beat. If you are a big dog and want to remain one, you can't rest on your past successes. It will serve you well to consider things from the perspective of the underdog from time to time.

Big dog, little dog, or underdog. Whichever one you are or aspire to be, use it to your advantage and always be the best dog in the fight.

CHAPTER 29
LAST IMPRESSIONS MATTER

TO SAY THAT EVERY INDY 500 delivers crowd-pleasing excitement is an understatement. While there are some races that are better than others, anytime you have 33 cars circling a two-and-half mile flat oval, two hundred times at speeds around 230 mph, you are guaranteed death defying thrills. Most race attendees focus on the cars out in front. But the experienced Indy 500 race fan knows that the true chaos can be seen throughout the entire race field.

You have past winners laying it all out on the line, hoping to taste sweet victory and sip the milk one more time. You have rookies trying to prove themselves. You have Indy 500 veterans, who have never won, trying to reach victory circle for the first time. The pressure from the teams, sponsors, 350,000 plus fans in the stands, and a worldwide audience of millions, forces these brave pilots to push it to the limit, and they do on each and every lap.

That said, having now personally witnessed over 40 Indy 500s, there are some races that are more exciting than others. For instance, Indy 2019, while entertaining, was not the most exciting for the casual fan of this great event.

Penske driver, Simon Pagenaud, showed up ready to dominate in 2019. He won the Indy Grand Prix, which is the road course race held on the storied grounds of the Indianapolis Motor Speedway that utilizes parts of the oval and it's infield as the course. That race kicks-off the start of the Indy events each May. Simon then won the pole position a week later for the start of the Indy 500 by posting a speed of 229.992 mph. On race day, he continued to flex his muscle by leading the first 32 laps of the race.

As the race continued, several drivers stayed with Simon. A few lead here or there, mostly due to pits. Simon dropped back to second so that he could follow the leader and save fuel by drafting. The general sense was that Simon had the winning car and was toying with the rest of the field. While it is fun to see a driver and team come in and show just how good they are by dominating the race, it can also make for a bit of a boring race, relatively speaking.

With just over 30 laps to go, most of the crowd was becoming shiftless. Simon's clear domination led the fans to the assumption that the race was not going to be a memorable one or one that would be talked about. There was barely any action at the front, where most of the fans had focused their attention.

And then in a moment, it all changed. Andre Rossi, who had chased Simon all day long, took the lead. At the same time, a big multi-car crash happened resulting in the race being red flagged (stopped). When the race went "green" with just 14 laps to go, Simon, as expected, came back around Rossi to take the lead before they even reached the first turn. This was exactly what happened.

What we did not expect is what happened next. Simon was leading, with drivers Rossi, Newgarden, Carpenter, Sato, and Power nose to tail right behind him. And they stayed there. Every one of these drivers had either won the race prior, sat on the pole, been multiple season champions, or all of the above.

For the next 14 laps, the race lead changed between Rossie and Simon on nearly every lap. The crowd, now on its feet, were breathless witnessing the shear tenacity that each of these drivers displayed. With just three laps remaining, it looked as though Rossi would win the race for a second time, as he passed Simon and pulled away. Adding to the tension, Simon found himself fighting with 2017 Indy 500 winner, Takuma Sato for second, almost falling back to third. With two laps to go, Simon somehow pulled away from Sato and swooped past Rossi for the lead. But this time he could not pull away. With just two corners to go on the final lap heading into turn three, Rossi went wide and pulled side by side with Simon. Simon went low and pulled ahead just enough to beat Rossi at the line by a mere 0.2 seconds – the seventh closest finish on record. Remarkably, Sato was just 0.2 seconds behind Rossi.

The crowd was spellbound. So much so, that the race became an instant classic and one that is still talked about to this day. Sports networks from around the world have since reported that the 2019 Indy 500 is one of the most requested races by viewers.

So how did a race that was not really much of race for most of the race, become such a fan favorite? Simply because people remember what they last see. That is why so many music acts save their best songs for the end of the show. It is why nearly every mystery movie waits until the last minutes of the film to deliver the big twist. In Alfred Hitchcock's movie Psycho, people don't talk about the entire film, they talk about the last few minutes when the truth about Norman Bates is revealed. That is what everyone remembers.

First impression are important, but no less so is the last impression. Audiences will most remember the last note. It is certainly what the fans of the 2019 Indy 500 remember. The first 186 laps may have been a bit dry, but the last 14 were classic Indy. Everyone who witnessed that race will never forget those last 14 laps. Simon fought fiercely in the closing laps to secure what was rightfully his. He left a last impression that made history.

LESSON LEARNED

You must never assume that just because you won someone over with a great first impression, they will remember you. While a great first impression is invaluable in capturing your audience's attention, you have to back-up that first impression with knowledge, meaningful presentations, and showmanship, if you wish to keep their attention. Beyond that, if you want someone to remember you long term, you must develop the skill of leaving a strong last impression. That last impression can include a clever remark, a reassurance of how your product is the best, or a kind gesture. How you leave a situation is most likely how you are going to be remembered. It's an opportunity you don't want to miss.

PERSONAL STORY

Shortly after attending the 2019 Indy 500, I received an invitation to speak at several large and key conventions in the automotive industry. Although I had spoken at these events over the years, this time was different. There were going to be two international committees at these events scouting for speakers to invite to future events. Unlike the United States, where many of these conventions have 40 plus speakers from just the U.S., the international events typically have five to ten total speakers. Half of these speakers are chosen from outside their country. These are prized speaking gigs that few ever have the opportunity to experience. To make matters more challenging, the U.S. events had the strongest speaker line-ups I had ever seen. Well-known, best-selling authors, presenters, and masters of the stage were all in attendance. Standing out was going to be tough. Speakers were going to have to be at the top of their game to stand out and be remembered. It was a tall order to hope to be considered for one of the international spots.

I knew going in that the subject matter I was presenting was one of my best. My content was spot-on, and I was confident that I would be able to keep the attention of my audience. The hard part was that I knew everybody else on the ticket would be able to do the same. I needed an edge. After having recently seen the 2019 Indy 500, I knew that I needed to close out my presentation with an ending my audience would never forget.

I immediately went to work and spent two months prior to the first event, writing, re-writing, and practicing my presentation to produce a one of a kind close. I arrived at the first event a day early and practiced my new ending no less than 10 times, recording it each time and playing it back until it was perfect.

I was nervous on the morning of the event. It is one thing to make a presentation that you have made many times before. You know what to expect. It's quite another thing to present new material for the first time. You have no way of knowing the re-action you will receive. I was stepping way out of my comfort zone and going big. This new ending was either going to blow the audience away or make me look like a fool. I felt as I imagine driving into the third turn of Indy would feel like, three cars wide. Three cars may be going in, but it is highly unlikely that three are coming out on the other side.

My gamble paid off! Not only did the new ending work, it also got me a standing ovation and a ton of inquiries from busi-nesses immediately afterward. I walked away from two of the events as the number one rated speaker. In the third event, I was ranked third. All in all, it was a resounding success.

I was not only offered a speaking spot at one of the in-ternational events, I was also offered a spot at each of the events. This happened because I had learned the value of creating an out-standing last impression. That was several years ago and to this day, I receive invitations to make presentations from people who were in attendance at those events. The number one request is for me to deliver the five minutes that leaves the audience with a last impression they never forget.

Points to Ponder

Most who are in customer service and the selling profession learn early about the importance of first impressions and how to master them. However, first impressions have a first cousin and that is the last impression. Last impressions are rarely ever talked about, and hardly ever mastered.

While first impressions are important, I find them to be more of a first perception. Consider your last impression to be like the dessert after a five-star meal. It's the finale. Great finales always leave the customer wanting more. More of your products, more of your services, and more of you.

The effort you invest in developing your final impression will pay you back a thousand times and make getting what you seek much easier. Your last impression should be one that lasts in the memory of your customer. Spend time figuring out how to impact your customer in a way that goes beyond your meeting with them. This investment will keep your customers coming back for more. Customer loyalty is rooted in making favorable last impressions.

CHAPTER 30
HISTORY MADE

LET'S REWIND TO THE BEGINNING OF THIS BOOK. You will remember that chapter one ended with three-time Indy 500 winner, Helio Castroneves, on the outside of Takuma Sato. They were on the front straightaway, inches apart as they stormed toward turn one with only two laps to go. Five years earlier, in 2012, Sato attempted a highly risky pass on the inside of two-time Indy winner, Dario Franchitti, heading into turn one on the last lap of the race. He met his destiny up against the wall in a hard crash. But this time, Sato had a slight edge. It was his corner, his race, and nothing was going to stop him. Sato was looking ahead this time. Coming off of four, he had anticipated that Castroneves would be there. By the time he found himself side-by-side with the three-time champ, he had already made the necessary adjustments to force Helio's eventual counter move. He was looking ahead and with only two laps to go, his eyes were already locked on the short chute between turns one and two. He was looking ahead to the final lap and looking ahead to the checkered flags and victory circle. He was looking ahead to taking a swig of the refreshing cold milk that is reserved for winners only. He was looking ahead because he had been here before. Five years earlier, he was on the offense, and this time he found himself on the defense. If Castroneves wanted his fourth Indy 500 win, he was going to have to risk hitting the wall. Castroneves always made the big moves and was not afraid to take chances. But he was a smart driver and didn't make dumb moves. He lifted for just a second, giving Sato the corner, just the way Sato wanted it. I am sure Helio must have been thinking that he could catch Takuma on the remaining two laps. But it was not to be. The one thing that Helio was not fully prepared for that day was Sato's determination. Coming out of that first turn, Takuma put just the right amount of distance between himself and those behind him. That move meant that it would take Castroneves the full two laps to catch up to him again. As they crossed the finish line and took the checkered flags, Helio was only a car and a half back. Sato won the race that day because Helio had mistakenly played it safe. Sato won because he was not going to lose. Sometimes drivers win because of other driver's misfortunes or because of other's mistakes. Not in 2017. Not on that day. Sato won because he was, mentally, several steps ahead of the other drivers on the final laps. He won, not just because his car was fast, but because he was looking ahead, planning where he needed to be. That day he was in control, and if someone were going to beat him, they were going to have to take great risks. As I recall, Takuma, the first Asian born driver to win the Indy 500, said in victory circle, "It's Beautiful!" That says it all. He was right. The fans recognized what he had done and it was indeed beautiful.

LESSON LEARNED

If you listen to drivers as they describe their driving styles at Indy, they talk about all sorts of details that separate them from the rest. They will try anything to win an advantage or go just that much faster. One thing they all agree on is where to focus their eyes as they drive the 2.5-mile superspeedway. All of the drivers will tell you that they lock their sight-line down the track to where they want to go. They don't just look in front of them like we do when we drive. They are always looking a couple of hundred yards down the track. If you ask them why, the general consensus is that they believe their mind and their vision will guide their hands to steer them where they need to go. It other words, it does them no good to focus on where they are. The reason is because they are already there. They need to look ahead and focus on where they need to go. They have to visualize and anticipate, using all of their senses, the next step in achieving their goal.

As looking ahead is crucial in race car driving, so too is it critical in business and in life. It does you little good to focus on the here and now. You need to project your vision toward the future so that you will be able to meet challenges with a well thought out game plan. It's too late to address the present. You are already here. If you are doing well in the present, good for you. But that is no guarantee that the future will bring you the same results. If you are having challenges in the present, the future is the only place where those challenges can be addressed. You need to plan and anticipate by having a vision that looks beyond where you are and focuses on where you want to be. Just like a race car driver, to get further down the track in life, you have to look further down the road and allow your mind's eye to guide you toward your goals. Simply stated, you have to know where you are going if you ever wish to get there.

PERSONAL STORY

When I was 18 years old, I decided to leave home and get married to my high school sweetheart. On the day I moved out, my dad sat me down and said the following, "I think what you are doing is a mistake. That said, I know you well enough to know that once you have made up your mind to do something, there is no talking you out of it. So, if you are going to go, take this advice - Go see it, go do it, and go be it! Whether you can do it or not all rests in your head." My dad told me that, to be successful, I had to aim high and work hard. I needed to focus on the big stuff and not sweat the little stuff.

But the words that stayed with me from that day and stay with me still have to do with understanding the difference between working for necessities and working for the things that truly give your life meaning. My dad believed that goals should never center around the necessities of life. Goals answer to a higher order. Goals are the bigger things that take you to your dreams. The rent and utilities, gas for the car, and groceries are all necessities. They are the absolute minimum of what you need to achieve for survival - food, shelter, transportation. Don't mistake the ability to survive with achieving a goal. You reach for goals. Goals require that you stretch yourself beyond the necessities of life. Our goals take us to new heights. My dad made it perfectly clear to me that chasing necessities would not lead to a fulfilling life. If my goals were solely to pay the rent, make the car payment, and fill the fridge, I would always be looking down, not ahead. I needed to pick my head up and look forward into the distance. "Goals are big picture stuff," my dad told me. He was right. Pursuing your goals takes you to big places. If you can achieve your goals, the necessities will take care of themselves. My dad was right. You should not be working to pay the rent - you should be working to provide for a meaningful life. Place yourself in the big picture. Set your sights high and work hard to accomplish your goals. Take my dad's advice and go for the big stuff. By doing this, you will realize your dreams and everything else will fall into place.

There is no question that my dad's advice was great. However, it wasn't until I was older that I started to do what my dad suggested. You see, at 18 I was smarter than my dad, and I did not heed his advice. I stumbled around for several years doing exactly what he told me not to do. I chased the necessities of life. I would visit the gas station two or three times a week, putting in a few dollars' worth each time. I never had enough money to fill my tank. I paid late fees on my rent. I ate cereal and grilled cheese sandwiches because that is all I could afford. I was working for necessities, and it sucked.

When I went to work for Bev at her furniture company a few years later, she showed me what my dad had tried to tell me many years before. It changed everything in an instant. She showed me how to find a goal worth working toward. She helped me find something to be passionate about. Nobody is passionate about paying their rent or buying gas. Once I discovered the magic of having a goal to motivate me, the goals became everything, and the necessities became non-issues. Suddenly it seemed like it took nothing for me to meet my everyday expenses. Today, the necessities have become an afterthought in my life. I am lucky because when I take my seat in that first turn at the start of the Indy 500 each year, and I see those cars come at me screaming off of turn four at a rate of one football field every 7/10ths of a second, I am reminded of why I work so hard and why it's worth it. I get out of bed every day, no matter how I'm feeling, and I get it done. It means working when I have the flu, enduring delayed or cancelled flights, fighting hard for every sale. It means giving my very best performance at every engagement and every workshop. It means working weekends when others are at home with their families. It means keeping my eye on the goal and putting myself in the big picture, and it is totally worth it. No question. I keep a three by five-foot picture of the start of the Indy 500 on a wall in my office, directly across from my desk. I see it every day that I am in the office. I have also snuck more than a few Indy pictures around our house as a constant reminder of why I am doing all that I do. Sure, there are other things in my life that I strive for and that I have set as goals. But going to the Indy 500 and watching that great spectacle every year is the prize that keeps me motivated. I would do just about anything to be at Indy for race day. When I daydream, I think about becoming a multi-billionaire, like Bill Gates. If I had that kind of money, I would buy the track and run that race at least once every day! Why not? You can take it with you.

Like Takuma Sato, I do not worry about where I am right now because I am already here. I keep my focus several hundred yards down the race track called life. Although I hit a few walls here and there, and I occasionally spin out, I never run out of gas, and I let my goals lead me to where I know I want to go. By doing so, when I get out of bed these days, I am not doing it to keep a roof over my head. I am not doing it to keep gas in my car or to feed my family. I am doing it because by working hard, staying focused, and driving toward my goals, I will be going to the Indy 500! I know to some of you this may sound a little strange, but it really makes all the difference. It puts a whole new spin on things. Silly or not, I got out of bed today because I am going to the Indy 500! Why did you get out of bed today?

POINTS TO PONDER

It is one thing to know where you are going, but it is totally another to enjoy it once you get there. So many times, I see people that feel guilty at work because they are chasing necessities and not working toward their goals. They feel guilty when they are at work because they think they should be at home with their families. When they are at home with their families, they feel guilty because they think they should be at work. If you are never at peace with where you are, then you are incapable of being in the moment. You cannot be truly present if you are conflicted. You have to be content with where you are and believe that where you are going is worth any sacrifices you make. Establish goals that you are passionate about, then prioritize your life based on those goals. When you do this, you will be on a much clearer path to believing with all your heart that you are exactly where you should be. There is no room for guilt. If your goals are worthy, you will feel committed to and satisfied with your life. Don't fall victim to focusing on the wrong things at the wrong time. Focus on work when you are at work. Focus on your family and friends when you are with them. Feel good about where you are. Create the life you want to live and live it. No regrets. No guilt. If you are doing what you truly believe in and looking forward, placing yourself in the big picture, everything will fall into place. Your life will be what you deserve. Nothing less than amazing!

FINAL THOUGHTS

So, we have reached the bittersweet part of Indy that I hate. The end always means a long wait until those 365 days pass and we get to do it all over again. These days, it is a little bit easier because of YouTube since I can go online and watch nearly every past race or portions of them whenever I like, and I find myself doing that several times throughout the year. It is kind of crazy, but when I watch these old races, they still spark many of the same emotions I experienced when I was there in the stands. There is even an added bonus: watching these old races not only does that, but they also bring back the memories of people and events that happened around a particular race, and that always cheers me up. They bring back memories of my dad. Memories of the time one of my favorite uncles, Uncle Bud, took me up on my offer and went to the race. What a day that was. Or the memory of a rainy day at the track where my brother Randy, my sister Esther, and her husband Frank, and I sat in Frank's old Chevy Van and drank so much that hours after all the on-track activities had been cancelled a security guard had to wake us up and tell us to leave.

There are so many more lessons and stories to tell. There were times when I would be at the track really early or really late and just happen to walk by a garage and get a driver or team own-er at the right moment and have hours long conversations. A.J. Foyt talked to me, just me and him, one morning for about 30 minutes. We didn't even talk racing either. The sole reason it only lasted an 30 minutes is because I felt guilty for taking his time and said goodbye. Arie, Al Sr., and Eddie Cheever did the same at other times. Eddie Cheever actually let me bring some business prospects to the garage one time and made me look important by taking 30 minutes to show them around the garage, the whole time acting like we were friends. His only request of me—donate what I felt I could to his favorite charity. When I embarrassingly gave him a check for few hundred dollars, he acted like and made feel like it was a million bucks. Another time my wife and I ran into Mary Hulman-George. She spent several minutes talking to us like we were long lost friends.

There was another time Gary Pedigo and John Barnes from Panther Racing let me trade some consulting work at Gary's Chevy store for a decal on Buddy Laziers car. I did about $10,000 worth of work, and they gave me a spot on the car that I know for a fact was a $100,000 spot. They let me bring people to the garage and let me be on the other side of the wall during practice. I took a lot of pictures, and they are some of my most prized possessions. Here is an almost Indy story. One time another local Chevy deal-er, Bill Young, had invited me to go with him to the Michigan 500. He had asked me because he wanted to go with someone that really went to the race track to watch races. He was as big a fan as I was. Of course, I said yes, and after I did he surprised me by tell-ing me that we would be flying to the event on Kenny Bernstein's twin-turbo airplane with the Budweiser Indy Car team. Yes, that Kenny Bernstein. Once up in the air, I guess I was looking a little odd. Bill looked over at me and asked if I was okay. Yes, I told him, but it had just hit me how unimportant I was. It had just hit me that if that plane crashed like small planes have a tendency to do, the headlines in the Indianapolis Star would read, "Budweiser IndyCar Team dies in fiery plane crash with prominent car Dealer Bill Young and some other guy." In every small plane crash there is always "some other guy," and I was him. My place in life was never more defined than at that moment. Bill just laughed and said that I was gonna feel plenty important when we landed. He was right. As we parked next to Mario Andretti's jet and deplaned, Mario walked over and talked to all of the team, Bill, and even me, making me feel as important as everyone else.

And that is what makes the Indy 500 and all of its players so cool. They always make you feel like family, like you belong and like you are the most important person on the planet. Everyone feels it. Even on race day with over 350,000 people on the property. You look around and see it on everyone's faces. They all feel important and are. They know that they are one of a very small percentage of people on the planet that get to be at the track that day, and they feel blessed and important because that is the way Indy treats you and makes you feel. From the top down and from the bottom up. Everyone is there not just for the event, but for the family, friends, experience, and lessons. I have told you about some of mine, and I hope you have enjoyed and benefited from the stories and lessons I have put forth. I hope that you too some-day get to go to Indy, and if you do or if you already have, I hope to meet you someday and hear your story. It is only fair that you tell me yours since I just told you mine. You know where to find me at least once a year. That place is the Indianapolis Motor Speedway every May on Memorial Day weekend enjoying my family, my friends, and most importantly, the Greatest Spectacle in Racing—The Indianapolis 500! I will be easy to find: I will be the guy in the Indy 500 tee shirt and hat, in turn one, Penthouse B.

Made in the USA
Coppell, TX
02 May 2023

16286939R00125